WHO CARES?

MY LIFE WITH TOM BAKER

COURTLAND D. LEWIS

kOZMIC PRESS

ISBN: 978-1-7340840-4-7

kOZMIC Press
www.kozmicpress.com

TABLE OF CONTENTS

INTRODUCTION

June 11, 2018 was a fairly typical summer day in western Kentucky: hot, muggy, and probably a few rain showers. The one big difference was that Tom Baker's *Doctor Who* serial "Genesis of the Daleks" was broadcast in local theaters. So, after enjoying a pleasant meal at a local restaurant, I sat down in the theater's comfy recliners with a "sonic screwdriver" and enjoyed the 40-foot-tall mass of curls and teeth that is Tom Baker. With glee in my heart, I thought to myself, "I'm going to write a book about Tom Baker." Of course, as I later sat down to begin the project, I thought, "Who cares what some random person has to say about Tom Baker?" Thankfully, my second thought was, "Who cares if anyone else cares? I care, and since I'll be the one doing the writing, ultimately it only matters if I care." Nevertheless, I would like you to care, at least enough to read the book. So, with that in mind, let me offer a short argument for why you should care and read this "random" person's musings on Tom Baker.

First off, I don't feel as though I am random. I have spent all but the first six years of my forty some-odd years of life engaging in the *Doctor Who* universe—the "Whoniverse." My time with *Doctor Who* began in 1983 and slowly grew over two decades, culminating in immeasurable hours of research (watching and reading *Doctor Who* is research!), publishing a book, several chapters and articles, co-editing two books, and making several appearances as a special guest at conventions and conferences related to *Doctor Who*. People enjoy my writings and presentations, so it's my hope that they will enjoy this book as well.

Regardless, like most books, this book is mostly for the enjoyment of the author. Writing is something an author does for her or himself. It is an added benefit if others like what is written. Don't get me wrong, authors love it when readers enjoy their work, but the therapeutic act of writing is first-and-foremost for the author. On a personal level, there are two reasons I started the book. First, the one thing readers most like to discuss from my book *The Real Meaning of Doctor Who* is the fact I drank kerosene when I was two years old. Sure, they have questions about the great philosophical insights into the Doctor's lessons on how to live our lives, but they're more captivated by the personal narrative. So I thought, maybe my next book should include similar life experiences? Little did I know that it would focus exclusively on them!

Second, as I get older, and the memories continue to accumulate, the crispness of the past slowly starts to dull. What is more, after recently becoming a father for the first time, I find myself reflecting on the aspects of my childhood that I most enjoyed and that were most influential. Besides a handful of others, Tom Baker is the person who has had the most significant impact on my life. It's common to hear people say that no one person can make a difference, but my life-experiences suggest otherwise. Tom Baker is a shining example of how one person—a stranger who has no awareness of my existence—can drastically affect the lives of others; and in a few years, when my son is old enough to understand his father's rambling stories, I would like him to know that he too can make a difference. I realize my son will have his own heroes and influences (his favorites are the Fifth and Sixth Doctor, so he's already wise), but it's also nice to think that this book will give him some insight into his "crazy" father. As for everyone else, you too should understand that you make a difference in the lives of others, just as others have influenced your life. So, whether you're solely a Tom Baker fan, a fan of *Doctor Who*, or you're curious about the author, my hope is that you all find inspiration, some humor, and most importantly, clarity and understanding of your own personal experience of someone who has shaped your life.

The second reason why I think people will care about the book is because it's about Tom Baker! Is there anyone more fascinating than Tom Baker? I do not think so, yet there are surpassingly few books on the man. Besides the autobiography *Who on Earth is Tom Baker?*, several *Doctor Who* episode guides/histories, and some nice featurettes, being a Tom Baker fan is slim pickings. Unlike William Shatner, there is no "How Tom Baker Changed the World." Sadly, I don't have the time or funding to complete such a project, but I am able to explain how he changed my world, helping me through difficult sad times and joyful successes. *My Life With Tom Baker* is an attempt to provide a playground for readers, sharing some stories that will hopefully spark a little self-reflection, several chuckles, and a new understanding of our place in the world, and even though the book is told through my stories, I never stray far from the man with the scarf. Like me, I encourage that you grab ahold of the scarf and enjoy the journey, learning about yourself and life on the way.

Before beginning the journey, let me lay out the framework of the book and let you know what to expect. For those who have read my previous work, you are probably expecting a deep philosophical analysis of Tom Baker. I hope you will not be disappointed, but this book will be more autobiographical and inspirational than philosophical. There will be deep philosophical insights, for I am a philosopher who struggles to not over-analyze things, but I will not craft arguments for why Tom Baker exhibits or exemplifies one philosophical concept better than another. My book *The Real Meaning of Doctor Who* is dedicated to providing such philosophical arguments, and if that is what you are looking for, I would direct you to it or one of the volumes on *Doctor Who and Philosophy*. In *Who Cares? My Life with Tom Baker*, I describe several important events in my life related to Tom Baker. Some of these events will revolve around the watching of *Doctor Who*, others will be related to reading books, and several will be events or decisions in my life that were impacted by Tom Baker.

Let me be clear, I have never met Tom Baker. It is one of my life goals, but I'm afraid at this point in my life and his, it will be a life goal that goes unfulfilled. I do not think it matters whether I've met Tom Baker or not. People write books all of the time about historical figures and ancestors who they have never met, and their stories are just as compelling as first-hand accounts. In fact, one of the things I hope people will realize is that we have the power to impact complete strangers and future generations simply by existing and engaging the world. We do not have to know someone to inspire them to greatness or to help them flourish. We simply have to work hard to follow our dreams, and if we are persistent enough, others will notice. We will not all be famous actors on brilliant television shows, but we can deeply affect others nonetheless.

Due to the nature of Tom Baker's life, as a well-known author and actor, the book will also contain a review of some of his major works. Again, I do not plan on providing an episode guide or encyclopedia of his work, but I would like to indulge in what might be called a subjective analysis of Tom Baker's work. In other words, I will explain what I think about some of Tom's work, relating it to my life, raising questions about its impact, and teasing out insights into the good, the bad, and the just plain enjoyable. Such an analysis will not be an exercise in academic acumen, but rather a fun romp down some of Tom Baker's life's work, both *Doctor Who* and non-*Doctor Who* related.

I have split the book into four episodes, with the first three focusing on how Tom Baker influenced the trajectory of my life in major ways, and the final episode providing the previously mentioned review of Tom Baker's work. For those interested in the life-story portion of the book, just turn the page and begin with Episode One: Genesis of a Child's Wonder. For those interested in the review of Tom Baker's work, you can turn to Episode Four: Reflections on the Work of Tom Baker. For those not interested in either, there's always Episodes Two and Three, which you're probably not interested in, if you don't care about the other two. I assume, however, if you've made it this far, you are interested, so I hope you enjoy what follows.

Regardless of why, I'm glad you are here. I have confidence that you will enjoy the journey, and maybe I'll see you at a convention soon. For those who are really brave, you could always sign up for one of my classes, or shoot me an email. I'm not too hard to find. Just look me up at my college.

Be well, and may you have many wonderful journeys!

EPISODE ONE
GENESIS OF A CHILD'S WONDER

ON THE EVENING OF SEPTEMBER 17, 1983, I sat down on my grandparents' linoleum floor to watch what I later learned was called *Doctor Who*. I was six years old and intrigued by something I had never seen before. My imagination struggled to make sense of this strange new universe, but little did I know, I was hooked. Up to that point, most of my television viewing centered around Jerry Lewis movies, *The Muppet Show*, *The Carol Burnett Show*, *Three's Company*, *The Three Stooges*, and *Different Strokes*, not to mention the many cartoons that flooded the airwaves of early 80's television. Of course, I had seen *Star Wars* and loved it, but there was something different about *Doctor Who*. *Star Wars* was flashy, well-polished, and full of special effects, but when compared to this "new, low-budget" show on the Public Broadcasting Station (PBS), *Star Wars* seemed kind of shallow. *Doctor Who* had a twelve-foot scarf, regeneration, tons of villains and monsters, time travel, and the greatest idea of all, a blue box that was bigger on the inside. To top it all off, *Doctor Who* had Tom Baker, who with all of his teeth, curls, and eccentricities, piqued my curiosity and took me on a journey that continues even after thirty years. Don't misunderstand me. I was not sitting on my grandparents' floor analyzing my love of genres and characters. I was simply enjoying life as a young boy, enamored with all of the imaginary worlds television offered; but I was also hooked, and returned each week for a new adventure. It was much later that I started to reflect on these experiences and ponder why I was so inspired. Through these reflections, *Doctor Who* stood out as a seminal moment in my life, one that shaped and helped me become who I am: husband, father, teacher, mentor, adventurer, explorer, etc. What stands out even more than *Doctor Who*, however, is Tom Baker. I love all of the other Doctors, from Hartnell to Whittaker, but it's ultimately Tom Baker who forever changed and influenced my life. I have written extensively on *Doctor Who*, but I now turn my attention to Tom Baker and the inspiration and influence he's had on my life.

Before getting too far down the rabbit hole, let me set the stage of my existence in 1983. I was born in 1977, and after about two years, my parents divorced, and my mother brought us kids back to Mississippi where her parents lived. My mother, Beti, worked as a teacher, and my grandparents—John and Pauline DuGard—raised us while she worked and went to school.

We were not well off, my mother's teacher salary was somewhere around $16,000 to $20,000 a year, my "father" often refused to pay child support ($100 a week for three boys), and so we were lucky to have a home and food on the table. We survived, and from my point of view flourished, because we were frugal, had an abundance of fresh vegetables from my grandparents' garden, didn't have a lot unrealistic goals, and I was blessed with a rich imagination that allowed me to enjoy what little we had—I spent hours under the kitchen table pretending it was a spaceship, which I still have in my kitchen. We also survived because my grandfather spent much of his time working multiple jobs: preacher, plumber, electrician, farmer, exterminator, locksmith, and I am sure many more. He would sometimes leave little packets of money at our home to help with things. I don't think he ever took credit for leaving them, but without his help, life would have been much different. He also spent countless hours taking me on jobs, hanging out at supply stores, and experimenting with food—Miracle Whip on black-eyed peas, Miracle Whip on toast, and sweet tea floats with ice milk were some of our favorites.

I sometimes hear people talk of growing up poor and how it affected their self-image and sense of worth—as though they are somehow less valuable because of their poverty. I never experienced such a thing. I knew others were better-off because they had lots of the coolest new toys (*Star Wars*, G.I. Joe, and Transformers), cable, vacations, a father who cared; but I never considered it a sign that I was somehow less of a person. It was just the facts of life, and though I'm sure others thought of us as inferior, I never considered money as a component of a person's worth—I still don't. Don't get me wrong, I wanted the things that others had, but I realized they simply weren't part of my reality. No matter how badly I wanted the cool, color-changing Zartan (G.I. Joe), every *Star Wars* figure, or LEGOs, it just wasn't going to happen. I once had a dream that there was a stash of figures at a local ATM, and the next time we visited that ATM, I searched and searched for those non-existent figures. Money would've been nice, but we didn't need money to go on hikes at the Natchez Trace Parkway, play games, or explore the huge empty boxes my Paw Paw would bring home.

As a side note, LEGOs always seemed like the "rich kids' toy." Those little blocks were (and still are) expensive, but with help from my mother, I once bought some LEGOs for a friend's birthday party—it was a police motorcycle set that reminded me of *CHiPs*. Instead of giving it to my friend (sorry Scott), I kept it for myself, at least until my mother found out what I did. I got in so much trouble, and it took me months to work off the money I owed my mother for *stealing*—and I didn't even get to keep the LEGOs!

For the most part I was satisfied. I had my bike (a Haro Master) and several toys, both of which I bought with my allowance ($1 a week, if I was good), some free TV channels thanks to the rabbit-ear antenna, and a ton of love from my mother, two sets of wonderful grandparents, and two brothers (even though we mostly argued). To be honest, we didn't always argue. We loved playing games. One of our favorites was to tie each other up and see who could escape the fastest. My oldest brother Philip would always win, and it wasn't until much later that I learned he used a knife—cheater! My other brother, Thor, and I spent a lot of time on our bikes, similar to the kids on *Stranger Things*, though we never fought underworld beasts. We mostly went swimming, looking for cool adventures, and tried to stay within our mother's boundaries. During the summer, we would drink Big Red at the Lewis grandparents in Indiana and play baseball. Back in Tupelo, we would go to the plant nursery, Doodies, for "slugburgers" (depression-era dough burgers made with meat, flour, and egg), or simply to Southern Pipe (a plumber's supply store), eat chocolate glazed doughnuts, and drink Dr. Pepper out of glass bottles. Later, with the advent of Nintendo, we spent a lot of time playing *Super Mario Brothers*, *Zelda*, and *Metroid*.

Vacations were for rich people! We took one vacation growing up, which involved driving down to Florida, spending two nights in a cheap room with a view of the beach (more precisely, the levee of sand that protected the hotel from flooding), and then heading home. I'm not complaining. I loved it. I still laugh at Thor's mispronunciation of "Buckatunna, MS." (I'll let you ponder that one.) It was a glorious vacation, which was only possible due to a generous credit limit on my mother's credit card. It was the type of vacation that makes you appreciate the realism of the Griswold family's vacation to Walley World.

We survived by living off of the necessities and made do with frozen dinners, sandwiches, cheap soda (mostly Faygo), and for dessert, ice milk, frozen soda, and cans of condensed milk—don't knock it until you've tried it. We didn't have central heat and air. Our home had one A/C unit that was strategically placed to blow cool air through two bedrooms, we had an attic fan that we couldn't use at night for fear of burglars, and we had windows, which again, we didn't use at night because we might get robbed. It wasn't that we lived in a rough neighborhood. My mother was simply afraid of being robbed, because she had experienced a break-in when she was young. With no windows to open, during the summer you just learned to deal with the heat. You either stayed outside or hoped you could lay claim to the coveted spot in front of the box fan, which had the added benefit of being its own form of entertainment, because it changed your voice when you spoke or sang. It's still fun to talk into a fan, if you've never tried it.

My grandparents had a window A/C unit too, but for some reason it was rarely, if ever, used. In fact, I kid you not, they often ran the heater during the summer. My grandmother would often use the heater as a substitute oven to cook potatoes, but everyone besides my grandparents felt as though we were undergoing a religious rite of passage to prepare and/or dissuade us from the torment of hell. We didn't have health insurance. Our goal was simply, "Don't get sick!" Thankfully, as a result of one or more of my grandfather's jobs, a local physician would give us free check-ups when we were sick. My biggest sickness was a recurring sore throat that would make life hell once or twice a year for about a week during each bout. We survived without cable. We had an old color floor set that picked up one or two local channels, and my grandparents had a similar black and white model. Even when they upgraded their TV, they still bought a black and white model. Funny thing is, I never noticed it was black and white until I was older. That was just one of those things I didn't notice because it didn't seem important. My imagination seemed to just fill in the gaps, as it sometimes still does. Regardless, TV played a central role in our family structure. We watched day and night, and so, I am not surprised TV played a pivotal role in who I became and what I do.

My memories begin at the age of two, when I accidently drank a large amount of kerosene. I almost died, and probably would have, if my grandmother had not looked out the window at just the right time. She was folding bedsheets and happened to look out as I began downing the coffee can full of kerosene. I was told she screamed, "Stop!", but I never heard her. She ran outside and began gagging me until the ambulance arrived. Her quick actions saved my life, though I don't remember much after drinking the kerosene. I don't remember the ambulance, but she couldn't drive, so I know of no other way I could've gotten to the hospital. I was placed in an oxygen tent for several days, in a comatose state.

Here's a part of the story I rarely tell, but since you bought the book, here goes. The doctors didn't expect me to survive, and even if I survived, they expected me to have extensive lung, stomach, and possibly brain damage. According to my mother, after several days of prayer, she saw an angel appear over my bed, then enter my oxygen tent and surround me with light. Shortly after the angel disappeared, I woke up, and I have never suffered any ill-effects from the ordeal. Crazy, right?! Well, if I were hearing the story, I would be skeptical too. In fact, I was there, and I am skeptical! During the ordeal I experienced something similar. I too remember seeing some sort of form floating over me, which then embraced me and I awoke. Was it an angel? I do not know. The skeptic in me says it was probably a mixture of the oxygen rich atmosphere and me waking up, but the visceral nature of the experience makes such an explanation hard to accept. What is more, my mother and I never shared our experiences until years later. So, our stories were not simply the result of storytelling in the aftermath of tragedy. I will probably never know the truth and nature of the event. My mother thought it meant I was destined to do something great for God's glory. No pressure there, Mom! For me, it served as a lesson on the fragility of life and not taking anything for granted.

As I note in *The Real Meaning of Doctor Who*, I recognized the same lesson in *Doctor Who*, and in the person of Tom Baker; and so, it is no surprise to me that they both played a major role in making me who I am.

After hearing of my kerosene adventure, often people say, "Well, that explains a lot!" I tend to agree. The trauma of the event jolted my mind into a higher level of awareness, while at the same time keeping me grounded in the wonderment of childhood. Being able to access my two-year-old memories has allowed me to retain the mental perspective of being a child during the most wondrous time of discovery. For a two-year-old, everything is a mystery and an adventure. Granted, I don't have total recall, but I remember things like navigating steps, early birthday cakes, toys and games, family interactions, and most importantly, my imagination landscape—the imaginative lens through which I understand the world.

I have always cherished my imagination. It has been my constant companion and helped me survive and thrive throughout my life. I don't know if it was the near-death experience, or just a short circuit in my development, but I have never really looked at the world as a static mass of inert matter. Reality seems too magical to be just be matter in motion. Reality is like a musical instrument: on the surface it's a block of hollow wood with strings, a tube with holes, a taut surface; but when engaged it becomes an infinite source of beauty, wonderment, and joy. Far too many people forget or never recognize the mystique of reality. Instead, they see it as an obstacle or an enemy to be battled. A child, however, sees the world for what it is: a process of becoming, a mystery of infiniteness, an orchestra of beautiful instruments. The imagination thrives when reality is properly understood, and it is this understanding of reality that I first recognized in Tom Baker and *Doctor Who*.

NOW THAT I'VE SET THE stage, let's talk more specifically about Tom Baker. Tom Baker was born on January 20, 1934 in Liverpool England. Based on Tom's own account, it was an interesting childhood with parents who worked—the father as a steward in the Merchant Navy and his mother as a barmaid and cleaner—and an extended family who came together to raise the children. Tom's deeply religious upbringing created a unique outlook on life that contributed greatly to his unorthodox approach to life. If you haven't read *Who on Earth is Tom Baker?: An Autobiography*, then you've missed out on one of the most enjoyable autobiographies ever written. To illustrate some of the quirky tales contained within its chapters, I'll share some stories that I find particularly important.

The book starts with the statement, "My first ambition was to be an orphan." Keep in mind that being born in 1934 meant that much of Tom's childhood involved the threat of Nazism and the eventual bombardment of England. Imagine growing up during this time. If you've ever encountered extreme circumstances like war or devastating natural disasters, you know how surreal life becomes. Think of the two Ninth Doctor episodes "The Empty Child" and "The Doctor Dances," and imagine a world where the rules, structures, and mores of society are obliterated. Such events create a disconnect between you and the external world—you know, that thing you never have to worry about because the world is reliable and dependable. When the world ceases to be reliable, our entire sense of self gets amplified and questioned. On a smaller scale, this sort of disconnect occurs when you travel—you experience new things, are put in awkward situations, and you learn a great deal about yourself and your understanding of reality and human nature. The big difference is that unlike traveling, which is often quite pleasant, war takes everything you depend on and violently rips it away, leaving you feeling lost and helpless. Whether travel, war, or something else, if we want to survive, then we must learn to cope.

Tom coped by praying that a bomb would drop on his "mam." It wasn't that he didn't love his mom, but he envied the presents sent from Americans to children who were orphaned by the war. Surely, Tom was not the only child to wish for such a thing, but what's fascinating about Tom is that he was willing to tell others about his wish. Herein lies the greatness of Tom. We all see and interpret the world in crazy ways, but most of us keep our "craziness" to ourselves. Tom, however, lets his "craziness" ooze from his inner core out of every pore of his existence. His look, voice, actions, and mere presence create an energy that affects the world around him. For some it's off-putting, for they feel as though he's aloof and unserious. After hearing Tom's wish, his childhood teacher accused him of wanting to be a murderer! For others, at least for me, it's a glimpse of an enlightened sage—someone who has broken through the barrier of the internal and external self, in order to create a cohesive being of Self. We're all capable of such a feat, but the constraints of life often make us fearful of making our inner self available for public viewing. It takes practice, and what we see from many of Tom's early experiences as a child is that he had a willingness to put his inner self out on display for others to criticize, reject, and as we see with his life as an actor, to love and admire.

I knew instantly there was an energy when I first saw Tom Baker on *Doctor Who*. He seemed like a true alien, and he showed me a unique way to live my life. I didn't grow up in war-torn Europe but would learn later that it doesn't matter where you grow up; what matters is *how* you grow up. It's always hard to talk about my birth—not because of some trauma, but because of certain location factors. You see, I was born in Louisville, KY, but my family lived in

Floyds Knobs, Indiana. Though I only lived in Indiana for two years, I grew up proud of my Indiana heritage: I was taught to love Indiana basketball, Bobby Knight, and the movie *Breaking Away*—a coming of age movie about a bunch of poor kids in Indiana who ride bicycles. Nothing strange so far, but things changed as I got older. After my parents' divorce at the age of two, we moved to Mississippi, eventually settling in Tupelo, MS. Due to my love of Indiana and need to explain how I was not from MS, anytime someone asked about my birth, I would (and often still do) dive into the complicated tale of how I was born in Louisville, but am technically from Indiana. Then the questions really began. Do you mean Louisville (pronounced Lewis-ville)? There is a small town in MS spelled Louisville and pronounced Lewis-ville, so every time I explained myself, they thought I was some daft kid who couldn't pronounce his birth-city correctly. I would then get self-righteous and explain how Mississippians lack the understanding of language to pronounce Louisville (LOO-a-vul) correctly. These conversations didn't go well, and as I grew up, I eventually learned that words can be pronounced in different ways, and that's okay!

The other question that created issues was, "Where at in Indiana?" I usually said Sellersburg, but no one had ever heard of the place. So, I would run the list of cities heading south of Sellersburg to Louisville. Clarksville? Jeffersonville? New Albany? Every once and awhile, I would get a "New Albany? I'm from New Albany!" The problem with this reaction is that I instantly knew the person was either not listening to me or was really bad at geography, because they had confused New Albany, MS (just north of Tupelo) with New Albany, Indiana—Indiana is not in Mississippi! Since no one knew of these *Indiana* cities, I created a go-to list of places that I used to experiment on people and their reactions: 1) I'm from Kentuckiana—the area where Kentucky and Indiana share large metropolitan populations around Louisville; 2) I'm from Floyds Knobs—no I didn't just make a perverted joke about the name of my father—By the way, "the Knobs" is one of the prettiest, nicest places on the planet, and is home to the wonderful Huber's Orchard and Winery; 3) I eventually, started telling people, "I'm from Indiana." Of course, now I live in Kentucky, where telling people you're from Indiana is sometimes dangerous, so I often cheat and say, "I was born in Louisville," being sure to pronounce it correctly!

Like I said, it wasn't World War II, but it was my own little war, and I had to make a choice about how I would respond. Like Tom Baker, I turned this awkward aspect of my childhood into a game, one that I was determined to never give in or surrender. As a result, I often set myself off as a little different from the other kids. I tended to be in my imaginary world, worrying and finding joy in things other kids didn't seem to know existed. Don't get me wrong, I had lots of friends, but I always seemed a little off from the rest. As

I grew older, I learned to accept my "oddness" and thrive on my own, never becoming reclusive but enjoying myself and my alone time.

I spent uncountable hours lost in my imagination, creating games and living out fantasies. One of my favorite games involved me knocking a tennis ball or racquetball onto the roof with my bare hand, gaining points when I didn't need any bobbles and losing a turn when it went to the other side or went into the gutter. The second game was a variation on golf, utilizing an old rusty golf club and a grapefruit-sized ball that washed up on the street one day. I would start in the neighbor's yard of my grandparents' home and attempt to knock the ball into the other neighbor's yard across a wide street. The course included a 90-degree dogleg, and the ball had to go in between two pine trees prior to going over the street. The final game involved me punting a football over a power line, while running to catch the ball before it hit the ground. I would play these games all day and into the night, until I was forced to come inside. I was good at them too! I can't tell you how many championships I won (and lost) over the years, but wherever the hall of fame for these games is located, you'll find my name listed as one of the legends. I would probably still play them all, but my roof won't allow it, my grandparents' home is two states away and under different ownership, and my body can't handle diving for footballs like it could almost forty years ago.

Nevertheless, no matter the circumstances, having a keen imagination IS THE KEY to survival. When reading about Tom Baker's life and thinking of my own, we wouldn't have made it without some sort of imagination to keep our minds active and to help us through difficult times. Of course, there are times when your imagination can get you into trouble, but without such an ability, we force our minds into rigid and sterile belief systems that make us angry, jaded, and miserable. Think of all the people who are angry today, living lives that seem meaningless apart from their anger. All they can do is complain about their lives and the people they think are out to "destroy" their way of life. I wrote and directed a short film called *The Meaning of Life* (https://youtu.be/MfKK1VkoDA8) with the purpose of showing the dangers of a life without an imagination. An imagination transforms the troubles of this world into something manageable and fun.

For me as a child, my imagination helped me overcome the existence of an oft-absent father, the tribulations of being the youngest child, loneliness when I felt lost, and peace when life was in turmoil. It allowed me to invent games I could play with myself. It turned trees into spaceships and time machines; it made bike rides adventures through unknown galaxies; it made cornfields, railroads, and graveyards battlegrounds for the forces of good and evil. In other words, it made life interesting, and when life is interesting, there is no time for being angry and hurt.

Tom's imagination made him an expert scavenger, and for anyone deft at scavenging, you know that it opens your eyes to a world that others mostly overlook or ignore. Like Richard Mayhew in Neil Gaiman's *Neverwhere*, there are some of us with an ability to see the magic of the world around us, where others remain lost in the fabricated world that society has created. A scavenger's eye kept Tom on the lookout for the strange and the unusual. It gave his life purpose, and developed the skill of observation that is invaluable to actors who need to be capable of mimicking personality traits. Couple his scavenging skills with his work as a lookout, protecting his mother's booking job from police intrusions, and you have the makings of an expert observer of human nature and personality traits. Both of these feed the imagination and influence how one approaches the world and treats the ups and down of life.

I was never a lookout for criminal activity (at least not when I was a kid). I, however, was raised to be a scavenger. My Paw Paw DuGard was famous for picking stuff off the side of the road and refurbishing it. My current TV stand is one of his masterpieces. He instilled within me the love of scavenging, and when people visit my home, I'm proud of the chairs, grills, tables, archways, and other "junk" I scavenged and made my own. He taught me to look for dropped coins and paper money pouches. I can still spot coins from almost anywhere, and will stop what I'm doing to collect my booty. When not scavenging, he would play games with what was readily available. One of his favorites was to find words in signs, bumper stickers, and the sides of delivery trucks and to scramble them to see how many different words he could discover. We used to spend hours battling each other to come up with words. There were no cell phones in Tupelo, MS in the early 1980s, and scrambling words kept us busy. I still do it when I find myself waiting for something to do.

Another important feature of Tom's childhood is his keen awareness of God's omnipresence—the theological belief that God is present in all places and at all times. As he discusses in his autobiography, upon hearing of such a belief, most people simply carried on with their normal activities. However, thanks to his overactive imagination, Tom was able to visualize the true implications of such a belief. If God is everywhere, then no matter what we find ourselves doing, no matter how intimate or disgusting, God is there watching. For Tom, this meant all activities in the bathroom and bedroom were viewed by God, which caused (and still causes) him a great deal of stress while trying to perform in both areas. I told you, having an overactive imagination has its disadvantages! Even with such disadvantages, Tom's belief in God shaped who he became. It created an ever-present force that caused him to be aware of himself. Such constant self-reflection results in a deep understanding of the world, and though it can make one moody and apt to brood, it also opens doors of perception into the dual absurdity and majesty of life. Self-reflection often sets a person up to be an outsider, even if they are surrounded by friends and loved by millions, because it creates a disconnect from the world. This disconnect has positives and negatives, but if a person learns to properly cope, they can flourish in ways that others seem incapable of flourishing. In Tom, it caused him to long for death, as a sense that life would be better elsewhere, while also finding joy in life. It led him to be a caregiver, but also to become an entertainer. It provided a space for him to take his loneliness, fear of God's presence, and sense of being an outsider and combine them into a cohesive and brilliant whole.

My early childhood was filled with church and God. Paw Paw DuGard was a Baptist preacher, so we were at church every Sunday and Wednesday, and often in between. As a child, I always enjoyed church and going to all of the special functions, like Vacation Bible School. This would change when I got older, as church became more about who you knew and what group was cool, but as a kid it was a place to fill my imagination. Hearing stories of how there's a God and that God became human to set us free from the chains of sin was (and is) infinitely fascinating to ponder and struggle to understand. I never had the fear that God was watching me in the bathroom, like Tom, but learning about God instilled in me a strong sense that the universe is too complex and fascinating for "this" to be all that exists. As with Tom, God would play a role in my life—sometimes in the negative, but mostly in the positive—for the rest of my life.

As a kid, I had no idea this was what I was witnessing when watching Tom, but as an adult, I see clearly that I found a kindred sprit (or spirit animal) in Tom Baker. Instead of bombs, I had a chance encounter with kerosene that shocked my mind into awareness. This awareness created a curiosity that was fueled by the many adventures that were part of growing up with my family. With my maternal grandfather (John DuGard), I got to go with him on jobs that required crawling under houses, visiting strange homes and business, going to hardware shops, and sometimes sitting in plumbing stores eating chocolate glazed doughnuts and drinking Dr. Pepper out of old glass bottles. I helped him farm corn, peas, greens, and all sorts of other vegetables and tagged along while he sold them to local vendors. I went fishing, snake hunting, learned how to pick locks, played all sorts of word games, and most importantly, listened to his stories of the past. It now sounds like growing up in a different galaxy, and for me, it kind of feels that way. I don't know if Paw Paw DuGard could sense my sensitive mind, but he definitely filled it with fun and excitement.

My other grandparents (Elliott and Nina) did much the same. Every summer, my brother Thor (David Thoreau) and I would make the eight-ish hour trip up the Natchez Trace from Tupelo to Sellersburg, IN with our grandparents, stopping often to eat, play, and enjoy the sights of the Trace. (If you've never driven the Natchez Trace, you should do it one summer. Don't get in a hurry, or you'll get a ticket. Bring some food, a sense of adventure, and be willing to stop often to enjoy the sights and the trails.) Summers in Sellersburg weren't just playtime. They had rules and expectations that we had to "relearn" every summer. Some of the rules were the same ones we had at home: brush teeth, wash your hands, etc. Others just seemed strange at the time: wash your face before breakfast, use tongs for ice, you can put your feet on the couch as long as you're not wearing socks, septic tank rules like don't flush the toilet at night, and among others, a complex ritual of using multiple forks and spoons to get butter and jam, so as to keep contaminants out. They make sense now, even though they don't seem to hold wives and grandchildren to the same set of rules, but at the time, Thor and I were constantly on edge of breaking every unknown rule. They also put us to work gardening, breaking beans, shucking peas, and doing all sorts of odd jobs. The strangest part of our visit, however, was they purposely softened their water. Again, it makes sense now that I live in the same area and suffer with dry skin every winter, but at the time it felt like torture. If you've never taken a bath or shower in soft water, imagine getting good and lathered with soap and having the water shut off. That's what it feels like. No matter how much water you use, your skin feels soapy and your hair feels oily. It was one of the worst feelings growing up, though it later served as a source of humor, because my brother enjoyed eating the little salt cubes used to soften the water—it's a miracle he's alive. I guess he was jealous I got to drink kerosene!

I'm not complaining at all. I always had a great time in Indiana. We worked and had rules, but we ate some of the best food and jams that have ever existed. We visited a ton of places, like Abraham Lincoln's boyhood home and the Louisville Slugger factory, went to Red Birds (minor league Cardinals) games, watched the Cubs on TV, and played yard darts (currently illegal), croquet, Rook, Euchre, and the most-loved Aggravation. I had several cousins who were fun to play with. Damon and I were always close, but Nat and I often butted heads until we got older, then we became close. Do not try this at home, but Damon and I would spend the summers mixing different substances in an attempt to make a "super-flammable" liquid. I think it was our attempt to be like MacGyver, but through dumb-luck or ineptness, our concoctions never worked. I sometimes wonder if Pap Paw Lewis found our concoctions and switched them out with something safe. He always seemed to be one step ahead of us in most things. We had some epic baseball games in the back yard, some fun neighbors, and a young woman named Rachel who would become my first girlfriend and first kiss.

Oh yeah, I almost died during one visit. If you're counting that's the second time I almost died. (There are a few more to come!) I went with my grandparents and cousin to Clark State Forest in Henryville, IN. After a picnic lunch and a demonstration of my surgical acumen at dissecting frogs, Damon and I set off on a trek to the park's watchtower. What kid would pass up an opportunity to take an unsupervised trip to a place where one could climb high, throw things, and possibly get into all sorts of other hijinks? The trek to the tower was much further than we anticipated, the stairs to the top of the tower were more numerous than hoped, and add to it the heat of an Indiana summer, we were not anxious to get back. In fact, we were secretly hoping our grandparents would give up and come get us in the van. Lucky for us, there was a "trail" of rocks that led to the side of a cliff. Finding my second wind, I jumped at the opportunity to follow this steeply inclined trail. In fact, it was my jumping that caused me to almost die. After becoming frustrated with the slow, cautious people in front of us, I arrogantly jumped past them; but once I jumped it was all "downhill" from there. My momentum forced me to either fall or keep running, and it was at this point that the blur of life slowed down and intensified the next few seconds into an eternity of life and death.

Here I am, exactly where I wanted to be: in front of the slow people, having fun, and headed towards excitement and adventure. Yet, as the momentum quickly hurled me towards the edge of a cliff, I realized an almost complete lack of control over my own life. My options were to fall on the rocks that created the path or run off the edge of the cliff. As life slowed down I realized I could try and jump to the side, hoping to land on a grassy patch. I decided against this option, because I knew I would never be able to jump beyond the massive rocks of the path. As I looked to the edge, I noticed a small tree with several leaf-covered branches. Quickly, I calculated my ability to use the branches to prevent me from falling off the edge vs. falling on the rocks. The tree option sounded good. I would avoid breaking my face and other body parts, and it would be like something out of the movies—I hit the limb, fly out a little, and then am safely returned to the ledge. Tree, here I come! My biggest fear at this point was losing the $200 dollars in my pocket that I had earned working for my father that summer. Looking back, with all of my wisdom as a logic professor, my reasoning was impeccable. *Star Trek*'s Mr. Spock would be amazed. Sadly, however, in all of my calculations, my impeccable logic was based on an ignorance of physics—mass times velocity equals momentum, and the momentum of a 180 pound teenager divided by a scrawny tree limb equals me flying off the edge of a cliff.

(Mandatory *Doctor Who* cliffhanger: I used to think a light outside of my bedroom window was an alien spaceship looking to kill human children. I reasoned that if I lay really still, they would think me already dead, so for several years, I faked death each night in order to avoid the child-killing aliens outside my window. Who needs monsters under the bed when there are aliens outside of the window? I'm going to blame my mother for the alien belief. We had a massive oak tree in our front yard, and she used to lament, "One day that big ole oak tree is going to fall on the house and kill us all." So, as I would go to bed and stare out the window, it was either focus on the oak tree that was going to fall and kill me while I slept or invent some other preferable terror. I chose the latter. As a result, bed-wetting became the norm. Better to wet the bed than to be consumed by aliens.)

The cliff! For those brief seconds, as my surroundings blurred, my legs struggled to stay beneath my hurling body, and I performed life-saving calculations, I found myself excited about reaching the edge of the cliff. Here is this magnificent tree limb that is going save me, allow me to have this exciting adventure, and to top it off, have a great story to tell. This is great! By the time I get back to the top, my grandparents will be there, my cousin and I will never mention it, and we will go home and have one of Mam Maw's epic dinners. The first sign of trouble occurred when the limb I grabbed began tearing and bending my fingers. For some reason, I was not able to grab hold of my lifeline. The second sign was the multitude of other branches that slapped and raked across my face. The final sign was realizing that my savior of a tree limb was behind me. It was at this last realization that time reasserted itself with a vengeance. Instead of the focused precision of "I'm gonna make it," life became the blurred chaos of "I'm gonna die!" Of course, I did not die, but my survival was the result of nothing I did.

The mountain edge I flew off was actually the steep decline of a small knob, so instead of doing a Wile E. Coyote and going "splat" after a dramatic fall, I did a sort of snowball tumble down the side. After the third tumble or so, I came to a rest. I was scratched, bruised, and missing my 200 dollars, but I was alive and as far as I could tell unbroken. I slowly got up, took my bearings, and started climbing my way out. At some point, my cousin (who thought I went to the great beyond) made it to the cliff and confirmed my continued existence. The pain and soreness was eased with the finding of my wallet and money, but was intensified by the lengthy walk back to the picnic area, heat, pain, and realized fear that my grandparents (Mainly Pap Paw Lewis) would probably achieve what the cliff failed to do—end my life.

I HAVE NO WAY OF KNOWING how much Tom Baker actually influenced my life, but as I reflect and interpret these experiences, I can't help but feel as though we shared a similar interpretive framework for life. We are kindred spirts, and understanding Tom's life helps me make sense and laugh at my own. Story after story illustrates how we both encountered unique battles, yet endured to enjoy (and hopefully bring joy to) the world. When I think of my protracted battle with bed-wetting, the shame, the strategies to overcome it, the late-night attempts to hide the evidence, I can now laugh, knowing that Tom too struggled and survived. I never thought I would stop sucking my thumb. No matter what concoctions my family tried, I kept sucking my thumb. It wasn't until I got deathly ill in (I think) second grade and blamed my thumb sucking that I finally gave up the habit.

I've never been prone to nightmares, but this one still haunts me. When I was in first or second grade, I had a dream that a man came through the window with the A/C unit and (I assume) did awful things. All I really remember is the man's face and him coming in the window and standing at the door to my bedroom. I don't know why the dream freaked me out so much, but it did; and I still get a creepy feeling when I think about it. What's even creepier is that when I got older, I met a man (more precisely, the man haunted me) who looked just like the man from my dream. I say he haunted me because one day (around 1991, when I was fourteen-ish) he just started appearing at a video store where I worked. Shortly thereafter, he began working at the video store. Then, when I quit and started working at Ruby Tuesday, he starting showing up and working as a dishwasher! We DID NOT get along, and I mostly blame the nightmare. Sorry Paul, but you were kind of creepy, and you scared me to death.

It's amazing how something so "minor" can affect your entire life, but this is exactly what Tom Baker did starting when I was six years old. My life with Tom began on September 17, 1983 with "The Sontaran Experiment," lasted through "Genesis of the Daleks" (September 24, 1983), "Revenge of the Cybermen" (October 1, 1983), "Terror of the Zygons" (October 8, 1983), "The Pyramids of Mars" (October 29, 1983), "The Android Invasion" (November 5, 1983), "The Brain of Morbius" (November 12, 1983), "The Five Doctors" (November 23, 1983), "The Masque of Mandragora" (November 26, 1983), "The Robots of Death" (December 31, 1983), and ended sometime in 1984, with several episodes I can't remember, except I know they featured K-9 and Romana II. (I know these dates because I visited the Tupelo Public Library in 2012 and went through seven years of microfiche—micro-photographs of old newspapers saved on film scrolls.)

Doctor Who kind of disappeared from our local PBS channel, so finding Tom was difficult. Every once in a while he'd show up on something different. I remember freaking out when he appeared in the *Remington Steele* episode "Hounded Steele" (1984). What a treat! It would be the last until my mysterious teen years of the 1990s, which are the focus of the next episode.

Tom played a major role in the genesis of my childhood wonder, and though I didn't know it at the time, as I look back on my life and that of Tom Baker, I see that it was our imaginations that helped us cope with life and even flourish. For that reason, I see nothing wrong imagining my life as one long journey with the legend and inspiration who is Tom Baker.

EPISODE TWO
REVENGE OF THE TEEN YEARS

I'VE NEVER BEEN CLEAR ON when you become a teenager, but I know it has nothing to do with your age ending in 'een'. If being a teenager means feeling awkward and confused, then it can happen at any time. In fact, I don't remember a time when I wasn't awkward and confused. I was taller than other kids, I wore glasses, carried my beanbag Kermit wherever I went, mostly wore sweatpants, and was, on the one hand, full of laughter and, on the other, vulnerable as a dandelion in a hurricane—meaning, I would cry at the drop of a hat if my feelings got hurt. To make things worse, me crying usually involved gasping for air at the same time, so ugh, I ugh, talked ugh, like ugh, this ugh. As you can imagine, I was the coolest kid in school…NOT! I was bullied and the girls stayed away, except for one girl name Stephanie, who I'm sure was either delirious or just loved sweatpants. Regardless, I avoided her advances because I wasn't interested in girls until around fourth grade—then I was the one who was delirious.

In lieu of these struggles, I had many friends. I was decent at sports and earned respect by being a class clown. The good thing about growing up feeling awkward and confused is that it's good training for being a teenager. To give a clearer example, when I was around five years old, my bother Philip took us swimming at his girlfriend's house. I didn't know how to swim at the time, but I knew the motions, and while trying to show my swimming skills with the aid of an inflatable raft, I tumbled over and sank to the bottom. Instead of panicking, I merely looked toward the shallow end and started walking—at least, I tried to walk. My movements were slow and tedious, and if Philip hadn't rescued me, I probably would've drowned; but as I think back, being a teen is exactly the same—you're suffocating, you feel awkward, your body and the world don't work the way they should, and without some sort of help, you drown. With that said, I place my arrival into the "pool" of teenage-hood around 1986/7, when I was in fifth grade.

1986 was a glorious year of girls, bicycles (I had a Haro Master), Poison, *Mike Tyson's Punch Out*, *Police Academy 4: Citizens on Patrol*, and all sorts of other discoveries. Nintendo was in full swing, I had my first serious crush on a girl, and I discovered the hidden treasures of the "fairer" sex. Late one evening, after carefully positioning the TV's rabbit ears just right, Cinemax (or skin-a-max) became just clear enough to bear witness to the strange activities of naked adults. Don't get me wrong, you couldn't see much, and I would remain utterly perplexed by the female anatomy for a least a couple more years (I had no idea girls had different genitalia than boys), but as Steven Martin says in *The Jerk*, "I found my purpose" that evening. Combine my awkwardness with a serious crush and a newfound purpose, and you have the makings of a dweeb-disaster. Her name was Hallie, and though I tried for years to woo her with my charms, she was sadly never interested. I pined, bought romantic gifts like heart-shaped boxes of Red Hots, and sang her praises to all my friends; but she made it abundantly clear that it was never to be. Grades suffered (I made my first D), friends teased, and on one devastating day, she put an end to it all. Hallie (and of course, all her friends and everyone else in the fifth grade had to come watch) confronted me on the playground and told me there was no chance of us ever being together, and that I should never talk of her, talk to her, or give her another gift. Looking back, I'm impressed by her fortitude, but on that day, I was defeated worse than the Cybermen in the Tenth Doctor episode "Doomsday." So, and instead of becoming a creepy stalker, which runs counter to the lessons of most 80's romantic movies (seriously, go watch a few if you don't believe me), I decided to leave her alone. I would spend the next several years loving her from a distance, secretly hoping that one day she would change her mind. Though I wanted to from time to time, especially after I thought I had achieved a minimal level of coolness in the eleventh grade, I never violated her wish to be left alone. Hope she found a great life, and that my advances weren't too traumatic.

Surely, Tom Baker never went through such awkward encounters—wrong! As we saw in the previous episode, Tom excelled in awkwardness, and his teen and early adult life were no different. Not to jump too far ahead, but since we're talking about the trauma of insatiable love for women, Tom tells the story of how monks deal with young recruits unable to control their bodily responses to lustful passions. According to Tom, there were certain monks put in charge of punishing those monks unable to control their arousal. These monks would bite the offending monk's protruding edifice, in order to dissuade such "un-Godly" behavior. As Tom notes, these monks gave new meaning to the saying "once bitten…twice shy."

It's this sort of approach to sexuality and bodily functions that keeps young people ignorant and contributes to the overwhelming awkwardness of being a teen. I never encountered a biting-monk (what a terrible monster for *Doctor Who*), but growing up in small-town Mississippi, my only resource for understanding the opposite sex was my mother. Upon watching my older brother have the "birds and the bees" talk with my mother, for many hours, I decided it was better not to know than to sit through the same torture. I kept quiet and self-educated, which as I mentioned, meant I didn't fully understand the female anatomy until sixth of seventh grade; but I faked like I knew everything, which only added to the awkwardness.

I open with this story because it seems to be one of the most consistent lessons in life: life is awkward and we often can't have the things we want most; and in the face of this reality, we must decide how we will live our lives. Will we persevere, and at what point does perseverance become obsession? Will we build a wall to protect ourselves from emotional vulnerabilities, embrace our fragility, become bitter, hate, dominate, self-mutilate, or just give up? Will we find others to love, will we trust them, or will we become so guarded that we are impossible to love? It's during our teenage years that we first encounter these questions, and how we decide to answer them determines a lot about who we become, if we remain immature and fill our life with distractions; or if we mature and learn to find joy in the face of harsh realities. This episdoe shows how Tom Baker and I answered these questions. So, I hope you're comfortable with awkward teenage stories, because for me, they're scarier than any *Doctor Who* monster.

DOCTOR WHO'S WILDERNESS YEARS, WHEN it was no longer aired on television, occurred between 1989 and 2005. My own wilderness years from *Doctor Who* occurred between 1985 and 1990. The world of a seven-year-old is full of many wonders, so as the sweet sounds of Van Halen's *1984* permeated the year that was 1984, it became harder and harder to watch *Doctor Who*. I was busy playing soccer, dreaming of running off with Olivia Newton-John, and becoming obsessed with music. By 1985, *Doctor Who* was off my radar, and would eventually become a mythological show that I wasn't sure ever existed. I asked friends if they remembered the show, and they would give me blank stares. I looked for the show on TV, and it was never there. I eventually assumed I would never see or hear of the show again. Remember, this is Tupelo, MS in the 1980s. There was not a lot of information regarding British sci-fi shows available, and there was no Internet. It wasn't until the opening of Tupelo's very own mall, "The Mall at Barnes Crossing," in 1990 that *Doctor Who*'s existence was confirmed. Contained within this glorious edifice to consumerism was a video store that had a small section of *Doctor Who* VHS tapes. Not only did I discover copies of several of the episodes from my childhood, but I also discovered specials and other tapes featuring additional Doctors, such as the First, Second, Third, and Fifth. They were expensive, but whenever I earned enough money, I would always go buy a video, until I had purchased all they had to offer. Most importantly, with my new discovery, I was reintroduced to my long-lost friend, Tom Baker, and regardless of whatever else occurred in my life, he has remained.

Tom Baker's teenage years centered on God and girls, and his stories of growing up in war-torn Liverpool, with its piety and oppression are eerie and shocking. For anyone who has never experienced a repressive religious environment and poverty, Tom's life is a case study for how one lives, thinks, and strives to survive. On the one hand, you're taught to be nothing. Any sort of pride or feelings of self-worth somehow diminish God's glory and make you a target of Satan. As a result, you are to be nothing, and if possible, less-than-nothing. As Tom proclaims, "*domine non sum dignus*"—"Lord, I'm not worthy." He was taught that the more you despised yourself, the better you were, and that when teachers caught him daydreaming, he would often reply with, "I am thinking of nothing"—if you're nothing, then you should only be able to think of nothing!

Emboldened by his ability to impress the pious teachers with his nothingness, Tom began immersing himself in religion. Since God loved sinners, Tom reasoned the more he was a sinner, the more he would be loved. So, he became an expert on classifying sin, and to ensure his sinfulness, Tom invented a criminal record for himself, which he then worked to convince himself was true. For anyone who has ever lived in a community that prided itself on sin, being a pious sinner is a dangerous game. It's like Monty Python's "Four Yorkshiremen" skit (give it a quick Internet search if you've never seen it), where each person tries to outdo the other in regard to how their lives are more awful than others. These "battles" can lead to some ridiculous statements, such as the closing one from Monty Python: "Right, I had to get up in the morning at ten o'clock at night, half an hour before I went to bed, drink a cup of sulphuric acid, work twenty-nine hours a day down [at the] mill, and pay [the] mill owner for permission to come to work, and when we got home, our dad and our mother would kill us, and dance about on our graves singing 'Hallelujah'."

Once you commit to being an unworthy sinner in a group of unworthy sinners, there's simply no limit to what you can claim to have done; for even if you lie about your sins, the fact you are lying only further confirms your wickedness. Once you convince yourself of your wickedness, then indulging in sin becomes easy—your indulgence only serves as more proof of your sinfulness! Tom started with creating a criminal record, which he quickly convinced himself was real, then he sat out to do some real sinning. You see, he heard there was a local girl who was rumored to do "it" for the right price. Like me upon watching *Island of 1,000 Delights* on Cinemax, he didn't know what "it" was, but he knew it was a sin; and that as a wicked sinner, he needed to make sure he did "it."

This is where flirting with sin gets dangerous, especially when most sins are associated with the things young boys find interesting. It all starts with the reality that life is tough. As Tom sadly admits, death sometimes felt like a welcome change from the crippling poverty of life. So, he looked for a means of escape, finding inspiration in the love and admiration associated with being a sinner. Stories of living within leper colonies even seemed romantic, until Tom wound up with scabies, and found no comfort from either priests or guardian angels. Such a spiritual reality check can extinguish the passion of religiosity from some people, but when life has little else to offer, people like Tom double down. He committed himself to the exciting life of the clergy, as a romantic mixture of farming, grape picking, and going to heaven; and in the process took his first step towards being a professional actor—while feeling the pain and discomfort of being a pallbearer at a miserable funeral, Tom's anguish was mistaken for grief and he received a nice tip. His first paid acting gig!

You might think the truth of some of his stories stretched too thin, but I can attest, as I grew up in a similar atmosphere, these are the types of thoughts and experiences you have on a regular basis. I loved heavy metal music, but because it was supposedly all of the Devil, with hidden backwards messages telling you to worship Satan and kill people, I tried to keep my love hidden. Everyone knew, and adults and peers at church would pray for my damned soul. Before I eventually accepted my love for metal, I would often try to convince them I wasn't that bad of a sinner for loving metal music. I once rewrote the words to AC/DC's "Hell's Bells" to sing "Heaven's Bells," because I was tired of being the focus of prayer time. Being a teen is confusing enough, but once you add sin, guilt, and a whole lot of uncontrollable desires, life becomes a minefield of uncertainty. So, you search for any available certainty, which for Tom was the clergy.

I found solace in simpler things. My favorite object in the entire world, and arguably my best friend, was a stuffed beanbag Kermit the Frog. Though he barely resembles a frog anymore, he's still displayed in my basement. We went through everything together, and it's amazing that he survived all of our adventures. There were some close calls, like when he fell down a drainage ditch, but he always returned home. Kermit was my own version of Woody from *Toy Story*, but I had sense enough to keep him—come on Andy, you're going to regret giving away Woody. As a child I carried him to school often, but even though I stopped when I became a teen, the stories of me and Kermit persisted, which means I continued to be made fun of for doing so. All of this teasing created an attitude in my mind where I stopped caring what others thought of me. As noted in the previous episode, I had an active imagination and didn't mind being alone. Learning to not care what others think, or stated differently, to be happy with who you are as a person, is one of the most valuable lessons of life. It's a survival technique that can help in almost any situation.

Like most teens, I eventually replaced toys with television, and the late 80s and early 90s were full of great TV. MTV played music all day and night, with special late-night programs like "Headbangers Ball" and "120 Minutes." *The Simpsons* began airing and were considered subversive by local religious leaders like Donald Wildmon (the founder of the National Federation of Decency), who loved to boycott Sears for supporting "indecent" TV programs. Luckily, my mother never joined their culture crusade, and let me watch most TV shows and movies as long as they didn't have nudity. So, just like Tom, I was instantly curious about nudity, and though I was convinced of its sinfulness, I also knew there was something important about becoming more acquainted with it. One summer my brother's Playboy magazine arrived when he was away at Boy Scout camp. Mother found it in the mailbox and went berserk. Of course, I was the only one there, so I was the only one who had to sit through several hours of her flipping through each page explaining why each image was sinful; then through the hours of her examining every cassette tape and VHS in the house for other sinful items. Many a tape was destroyed by my mother's hammer that day. I'm proud to say, none of my music was destroyed—not that I didn't have sinful metal music; I was just better at keeping it hidden. How? It's easy to exchange the tape from an "evil" Dio cassette into something less sinful, like The Monkees. With all of this drama telling me that everything I like is a sin, I dreamed of a different life, but unlike Tom, I never thought joining the clergy was the answer. Instead, I dreamed of being a rock star!

Even my rock star dreams were a little confused. On the one hand, I idolized David Lee Roth, while on the other, I longed to be part of The Monkees. I would never lose my eclectic taste of music, and by 1987 I was a full-on headbanger. Iron Maiden, Megadeth, Dio, Anthrax, Motley Crue, Led Zeppelin, Rush, KISS, and many more were constantly playing on my Sony Walkman or simply in my head—they're still constantly playing in my head. I was truly addicted to music, from Robert Johnson and Muddy Waters to The Cars and The Cure. I couldn't get enough, and if you lived through the 1980s you probably can guess what happened next. Thanks to some knucklehead preachers who proclaimed all rock-n-roll is of the Devil, full of backwards Satanic messages, and knucklehead music fans who blamed the Devil's messages for their bad behavior, my mother was convinced that I would be a Satanist killer if I listened to the "wrong" music. So when she found the sheet music for Metallica's *...And Justice for All*, she went through each lyric explaining its "Satanic message," then tore the book to shreds. Again, I was a much better hider than my brother. My nightstand and chest of drawers contained my whole collection. I found that beneath the drawers was just enough room to fit a cassette, so I filled them with my favorite bands, neatly alphabetized and placed in order of release date.

Sadly, Tom Baker has never recorded a metal album, though he provided a voiceover for the band Ayreon, so it's hard to compare the two; but before I move on, let me mention a couple of musical acts that are comparable in inspiration to that of Tom. First, no other musician has shaped me more than Bob Dylan. While riding home with my mother one evening, "Like a Rolling Stone" came on the radio, and I was mesmerized. We arrived home before the song finished, I ran inside to finish the song and pray they would say the artist's name. They did, and it was Bob Dylan. His music and lyrics rewrote the way I saw the world. Second, and closely related, the Grateful Dead helped me expand my mind into new areas of blues, jazz, and improvisation. Jerry Garcia's guitar work has always been air conditioning for the soul, and it's no surprise to me that after I finished high school, I followed the Dead until Jerry's passing. Finally, from the moment my friend Matt gave me a copy of *Dressed to Kill*, which he found abandoned in his yard, KISS has been a much-loved obsession. (Speaking of Matt, his parents were on par with my own. Upon finding their son influenced by metal music and other sinful things, they shipped him out of town to a Christian school in North Carolina. When he turned 18, I'm proud to say I went and "broke him out." To my mom's credit, she supported the act and let him stay at our home.) I don't care about people's complaint that KISS's music is shallow or that they are "Knights In Satan's Service." KISS taught me to be proud of who I am and to work hard to achieve my dreams. They remain a constant motivation for working hard and having fun. I've seen them eleven times, went with my wife and two-year-old son to their End of the Road farewell tour, and edited the book *KISS and Philosophy: Wiser than Hell.*

You might be wondering: where was Tom Baker during this time period? Tom wasn't around for my early teen years. In fact, as said before, there were times in which I thought I might have imagined *Doctor Who*. My mind was pretty full of fantasy. I had to keep track of all the games mentioned in Episode One, and sometime around 1986, I created an alter-ego as a rock star, which would eventually evolve into GLISS—an entire band, with personalities, touring schedule, and recording sessions. GLISS was a not-so-subtle reference to KISS, and after a few years, I discovered the word 'bliss', and retroactively changed the name of the band. Truth be told, I still actively imagine my life with BLISS, along with another two bands, all of which have separate members, solo projects, and your typical rock star problems. I used to worry that people would think I was crazy for having so many personalities together in my head, but when I think of the things others choose to fill their heads with, I find myself quite comfortable with my bands, sci-fi fantasy, and other imaginary mental landscapes.

To reiterate, it's this "craziness" that feeds my love of Tom Baker. When you read about his survival into adulthood, and even throughout his adult life, his craziness is what kept him calm, sane, and aware enough to "keep walking towards the shallow end." Of course, you don't always know which way the shallow end is. Tom thought he would be a monk, but he had too many questions, enjoyed life too much, and had too much of an active imagination to focus entirely on worshiping and serving God. As a result, the one place in which he found comfort escorted him from the premises and left him alone on the side of the road in tattered clothes. The public humiliation and shame of being kicked out of the monastery was only softened by the unyielding love of his mother, who accepted him back home.

I HAD A STABLE HOME, WITH no desire of becoming a monk. As previously mentioned, my biggest struggle was girls. I was more knowledgeable of girls than Tom, but I think that only made things worse. The problem was (at least how I understand it, and I have pictures to support my hypothesis) I had no style, no groove, was too dorky, poor, ugly, or whatever it takes to spark the interest of girls. I already mentioned Hallie, but besides her, I was girl crazy. My heart ached for Hallie, but the rest of me was interested in about five other girls. I would eventually date an out-of-state girl for a week or so, which of course no one believed. In eighth grade I dated a younger seventh grader named Amy. We dated for several months, which was an eternity in the eighth grade. We would date and remain friends for many years, until eventually life took us down different paths. She went on to become a famous fashion model—super proud of you, Amy. Before she would go on to be world-famous, we would get our parents to drop us off at the mall (just like you see in *Stranger Things*), and if she had to work, I would visit her at Bumpers, a Sonic-type place with good fish fingers. We had lots of fun, never fully admitting to ourselves how much we liked (loved?) each other, or was it never being fully ready to commit at such a young age? Who knows?

She was an important part of my teenage life that was enjoyable, and her friendship caused some tensions with my next serious teenage girlfriend, Chanda. Chanda and I dated for a year or so, thinking we would be together forever. We might have stayed together, but her mother didn't seem to be a big fan of me, and after she discovered Chanda's diary, we were banned from ever seeing each other again. (I'm not going to talk of what was in the diary, since it wasn't mine, sorry.) We secretly dated for a short time after that, but Amy and I were hanging out and rumors were spread. Amy was seeing someone else, and we agreed that for us to be together we would need to break it off with our significant others. Eventually, we tried getting back together but everyone else felt like they needed to get involved, and the drama of high school kept us apart. We still had fun talking and hanging at the mall, and I fondly remember seeing her one last time before heading to New York for her fashion career. Chanda and I went our separate ways, talking a few times over the years, until eventually losing contact with one another.

I guess most people's lives are full of random events as they slowly mature into adulthood. After Tom's dismissal from the monastery, he found work any way he could. Spent some time as a delivery man, as a barkeep, and with unceasing energy, kept an eye open for other jobs. It was during this busy time in his life that he was conscripted to the Royal Army Medical Corps. As a member of the Corps, he was put in charge of emptying and cleaning bedpans. There is no glamor in such a job, but it's full of valuable lessons dealing with one's own internal understanding of existence and lessons dealing with human nature and emotions. He learned to engage and deal with infirmed people, which provides insight into the human condition. All actors need some sort of insight into humanity, if they are to convincingly play complex characters. Cleaning bedpans surely gave him motivation and inspired a type of wisdom and humility to enjoy life, especially life-pursuits unrelated to the drudgery of his "day job," like acting. Eventually he was "promoted" from humans to cleaning up after pigs, which provided him enough free time to audition for a small role in local play. He was given the part of a priest, but during the first rehearsal, as he delivered a self-prepared sermon, Tom was fired. Instead of mumbling a few lines about God and Mary, he created an elaborate schtick, which flummoxed the other actors. To some extent, and he admits it later in his autobiography, Tom never learned not to steal the show. He sometimes got lost in the stage conducted in his own head. Some actors and directors love this sort of spontaneity, others despise it. It was the latter in this instance, but even though the director gave him the sack, he would eventually set Tom on the right track. Before saying goodbye, the director let him know that besides being "absolutely bloody terrible," he felt Tom had something that might actually work, if someone would take a chance on him. Thankfully, several people would eventually give him a chance.

Because of the awkwardness and craziness of adolescence, one of the greatest things that can happen to a young person is for an adult to believe in you, to give you a chance, or to say something positive. Such events don't magically make everything better, but they plant seeds in your psyche that allow you to put the pieces of life back together and to find focus in the middle of life's hurricane. Even though much of Tom's life was a "failure" up until this point, he left the Corps with a belief that he could act, and it's this belief that started him down the path of becoming one of the most beloved actors in history (and, of course, becoming my companion).

LIKE TOM, I STAYED BUSY working different jobs and looking for my place in life. My earliest job was selling designer pencils and other stationary in the fourth grade. There was a company that would send you a magazine, then you would go door-to-door selling different sorts of cutesy office supplies, and you got a cut of the sales. It was fun, but I didn't make much money. The real money came from the pencils my aunt used to bring me every few months. I would then take them to school and sell them to other kids. I would wheel-and-deal until my pockets were full of coins and sometimes cash.

Before long, I created my own landscape service, which lasted several years, until I dated Chanda, whose parents owned a video store. Sitting in a video store and watching movies all day sounded a lot better than melting in the merciless summer heat of Mississippi. Since there were not limits on what I could watch, I spent many days re-watching my favorite *Doctor Who* episodes. Only one customer ever recognized what I was watching and that was because he remembered K-9 from when he was a kid. Another guy went to elaborate means and stole my watch, which he thought was a real Rolex. No, it was just a $5 knock-off, but because he went to so much trouble, I had fun harassing him (or more precisely, his family) about videos. I would call and leave messages on the family answering machine, telling them he had never returned his super-XXX-taboo movies. I never got my watch back, but I got a bunch of laughs out of it.

My video store days came to an end when Chanda's diary was found, but luckily, I was old enough to bus tables at Ruby Tuesday (a restaurant in the mall) where my two older brothers worked. It was a glorious place to work. I was one of the youngest people there, but entered with a lot of street-cred because of my brothers. I would eventually master bussing tables, serving, being the "dishmaster," prep work, and line cook. By the time I was 16, I had restaurants fighting for my services. Though I worked at several, Ruby's was my favorite. It was not always easy, and I developed some bad habits for coping with depression that I would have to break later in life. For the most part, however, it was hours of hanging with my friends, and for anyone who has worked in the restaurant business, there's a certain excitement and power that comes from surviving the trenches of food-service-warfare. I'll talk more of restaurant life in the next episode, but for now, all I wish to say is that Ruby's was my sanctuary, and I still have vivid dreams of working there from time to time, and I cherish them all.

What's more, working at Ruby's gave me the money to buy my first car, an Isuzu pick-up, and buy all the CDs I wanted. I still have thousands of CDs, and it all started while working at Ruby's, where I could get off work, walk down to Disc Jockey, and buy anything I wanted. As previously mentioned, I was also (and still am) a mallrat. When I was a kid, we would sometimes drive to Memphis, TN or Jackson, TN and visit their malls. These glorious edifices to consumerism are still shrines of joy. I know many of them are dead or dying, but no matter where I visit, I want to go to the mall. They have everything: space, people-watching, comics, music, arcades, food...what's there not to love? When Tupelo got its mall, it transformed my life. I would spend every weekend, and any other day I could, hanging in the mall. In addition to Ruby's, I would eventually work at a music store in the mall, which gave me even more freedom to explore these temples I love. When I lived in Knoxville, TN and Birmingham, AL, both had a thriving mall scene, which makes me hopeful that the glory days of mall-life will return.

Malls weren't the only place to relax, hang out, and talk to girls. I spent most of my summers in Southern Indiana and sometimes Virginia. With the help of cousins, I tried meeting new girls, but they were mostly just amazed I had shoes. You see, they thought people from Mississippi lived in swamps, rode airboats, and didn't wear shoes. I wish! I still had fun and learned a lot about how to talk to girls, which got me good and nestled into the "friend zone." Though sometimes annoying, the friend zone taught me how to talk and listen, which I would eventually realize was more important than the carnal desires of a fifteen-year-old.

Another fun place to visit was the Friday night football games. Tupelo High School football was big stuff, and before they built a new high school, games were played on a field that was dug out of the side of hill. It created a neat environment to watch football, flirt with girls, and sometimes get in a fight (or try to avoid one). The stadium was near to the "bad" part of town, so there were always rumors of drugs and gang violence, which made parents declare certain places off-limits. I never had any luck with girls, but I was part of a couple of harmless scuffles, and I once had a gun pulled on me in one of the off-limits places. I guess parents sometimes do know best. Nevertheless, it made for a great story that added to my street-cred. To be honest, it wasn't that big of a deal. There was a set of trees close to a fence, where people would sneak in or sneak other contraband through the fence. One night, I stood guard while two guys jumped the fence. After the first one made it over, I was going to leave; but he raised his shirt, showing a gun, and told me to stay still until after they left. Afterwards, I told everyone the same story, except that he pulled the gun and threatened us to stay still or else. It wasn't much of an embellishment, but my classmates liked it and wanted to hear more. In other words, it got me some attention, and I liked it! Keeping with the theme of Episode One, I count the gun incident as a time when I almost died, because deep down I'm still that teenager who wants attention—though I think I've become a little wiser.

THROUGHOUT ALL OF THIS CRAZINESS, there is a deeper and darker side to being a teenager. After breaking up with Chanda, I felt a deep absence. It was as if my arms and chest constantly ached. Don't misunderstand me, it's not as if I was some lovesick puppy. Like Data, from *Star Trek: The Next Generation*, I was experiencing the loss of a relationship for the first time, and there was an adjustment period of figuring out how to cope. I filled the absence with minor criminal behavior, like dragging garbage cans down the road from a car window then letting them go, smoking, and eventually drinking and smoking marijuana. These pursuits seemed adventurous, made me forget the awfulness that I felt was my life, and made listening to music and watching *Doctor Who* more "interactive." They were, however, only attempts to escape the pain of feeling alone, as though no one loved me, losing my dearly loved grandfather, and a general depression that made life miserable. I often thought of dying and once held a knife to my arm, with the intention of ending it all.

Like Tom, companionship seemed easy on one level, but disastrous on another. The best way I can describe it is that it's like being an extrovert who is capable of jumping into any situation, making people laugh and enjoy themselves; yet, like an introvert, you constantly feel the need to be alone in order to "recharge." If you can't recharge, you have to find other means to cope with the crippling anxiety that is begging you to find a safe place away from all other humans. As a result, it's easy to make lots of acquaintances, but it's extremely difficult to maintain friendships, because you often disappear for long periods of times, which others translate as you not caring. I don't know if this is the psychological turmoil Tom experienced, but from what he says of former lovers and friendships, he seems to suffer from something similar to what I'm trying to describe. In *Who on Earth Is Tom Baker?*, he says, "I'm afraid I have no gift for friendship. I quickly get tired of people and off they go." He finds it difficult to think of old and current friends. It's easy for the skeptic to say, "Come on, this is Tom Baker; he has millions of friends." The skeptic would be correct, but the statement misses the point. Life teaches us strategies for dealing with others, and Tom's life taught him certain strategies of escape, which fans of Tom are aware of how during interviews it's never clear if you're talking to the "real" Tom Baker or the personae Tom Baker. Tom seems to have found a way to deal with the tension of friendship, which all must do at some point; and whether you realize it or not, our coping mechanisms start during the awkward and confusing times of being a child/teen.

I never went through with my attempt to escape, choosing instead to numb myself with chemicals, and as a result it took me many years before I found positive outlets for my pain and talents. Whether working at a restaurant, at school, or hanging around doing nothing, I was constantly in an altered state. I was miserable and didn't know how to cope. I would eventually go to college at the University of Southern Mississippi, in Hattiesburg, MS, but my destructive behaviors meant I didn't take it seriously. Instead of taking the opportunity away from home to find "a new hope" and positive coping mechanisms, I slipped back into depression. Life just seemed to suck. I felt forced to work, which kept me from following my dream to be a professional soccer player, I didn't recognize the fun and challenge of academics, and girl troubles continued. I don't regret these times. I met a lot of people and had a lot of fun, KISS reunited, and thanks to my carefree ways, I was well-liked and respected. I needed respect, and their respect would help me discover some interesting truths about myself.

Before I could discover these truths, I would have to discover some more self-induced hardships. In Episode One, I talked of how I almost died a few times. Well, not much changed as I got older. Dropping out of college at USM, I had to move back to Tupelo, which means I was going to have to move back in with my mother. The one advantage, I no longer hid my tapes or my substance abuses. During one of my trips moving to Tupelo I stayed up all night dancing at several clubs. At some point around four in the morning, I packed up my stuff, and with snow starting to fall (a rarity in Southern Mississippi), and against the protests of friends, I started driving home. Somewhere around Heidelberg, MS, listening to Bod Dylan's *Blood on the Tracks*, I fell asleep and my truck went off the road and down the hill of an overpass. I slept through the event but awoke when a stranger stopped to ask if I needed help. I should've been dead, but there was a fence that had wrapped itself around my truck and prevented it from flipping or running into any other objects. She went and got help, while I cut the fence from my truck. Help arrived to push the truck out of its ruts, and I quickly escaped the scene and continued to Tupelo.

I could have killed my friend Justin, who was riding in the passenger seat. I could've killed anyone else out that morning. You get the picture, I hope. I was stupid and it was dangerous. It taught me that I had limits, and it reminded me of how I once had a vision to do something important with my life, not just waste it away. It would take many years to right the ship, and it began with a movement towards finding a place away from my personal torments of life.

Like Tom, who was given positive encouragement from a director and was loved unconditionally by his mother, I had several people plant seeds of love along the ways. My friends saved me from "drowning," like Thor, Philip, Spence, Matt, Tony, Justin, Chris, John, Josh, Jason, Eric, Mike, Ben, and so many more all played their role in helping me live and be successful. I also had several adults love and encourage me, like Randy, my shop teacher for many years in high school, and mentors like Paula, my teacher and friend when I started back to college. Adults give you the wisdom to avoid falling into the water in the first place. Unfortunately, the only way some of us learn is by falling in a few times. Then the lessons learned from adults and friends really start to make a difference in our lives.

Wish I had known it then, but much of surviving one's teenage years is the same as surviving into adulthood—stay focused on what's important and never give up striving for your goals. When I listen to Peter Gabriel's song "Come Talk to Me," I often long to return to the days of watching *Doctor Who*, *The Muppet Show*, *Three's Company*, *Samford and Son*, *The Carol Burnett Show*, and *Mamma's Family*. Yet, we can never physically return to our childhood. Even if you had a time machine, you'd still be an adult-you disconnected from the child-you. Nevertheless, it is important that we're able to identify when we were most happy in life. Identifying these moments helps you both remember what made (makes) you happy and the dream(s) you had for your life. Once you've remembered what makes you happy and the vision you had for your life, you have the knowledge to take control and direct your life in the right direction.

I've found that Tom Baker and *Doctor Who* provide time machines that allow me to taste the joys of when and where I was most happy as a child. They let me remember when life was awkward and confusing, helping me laugh at how foolish I was, and that it was okay to be foolish. The ability to laugh at oneself is a sign of wisdom, one that gives me hope for a brighter future. With the next episode I will attempt to explain how I used this wisdom to flourish as an adult, where my adult-self and inner child-self delight in a world full of ups, downs, and sometimes the same awkwardness we experienced as teens.

EPISODE THREE

THE TERROR OF ADULTHOOD: FULL CIRCLE TO CHILDHOOD

TOM BAKER'S LIFE REMINDS ME of the Fyodor Dostoevsky tale *The Brothers Karamazov*. If you've not read it, it's a story that follows the lives of the Karamazov brothers and their unruly father. It's full of philosophy, theology, estranged relationships, the randomness of life, madness, and the existential angst that surrounds the mundane and meaninglessness of our existence. You can read it and be depressed by its awful depiction of humans or read it and be inspired by the richness of questions raised dealing with how we approach our own lives. I suggest the latter. You'll never make it through the book, nor life, if you let depression rule your interpretation of either. Tom's life is the same way. When reading *Who on Earth is Tom Baker?* you can either ignore or embrace the brutal honesty of how a life well-lived takes you in many strange, wonderful, and often contradictory directions. Your choice to ignore leads only to your own peril, while a willingness to engage and learn offers hope for a life full of flourishing.

Episode One of this book was about using your imagination to not only survive but also to thrive as a child and adult. Episode Two discussed the awkwardness and confusion of being a teen, and how, with a little help from friends and mentors, you might just survive into adulthood. Episode Three's goal is to bring these two lessons together and help you see that the goal of life is to take all the lessons you've learned while becoming an adult and to apply them to living life as an engaged "child." Let me briefly explain what I mean.

The world often teaches that your goal should be to grow up, get a job, and act like an adult. These are good goals, if your only goal in life is to be a good worker. Humans, however, do not live by bread alone. A fundamental aspect of being a human is that we are creative beings. We feel lost and empty if we do not have some sort of creativity in our lives, whether that's building a home, painting a picture, or simply doing the things in life that bring us joy. If you're lucky, your job will provide an outlet for creativity; but due to the nature of our society, most people end up in careers they hate, which then spills over into their private lives, ruining relationships and making them miserable. I spent ten years in the restaurant business, and I love to cook; but after a while, I became so alienated from my own work that I hated cooking, hated customers, and hated holidays, since I spent most of them cooking for customers. One day, after having an anxiety attack that left me crying behind a dumpster, I decided I would set myself free from being a "good" worker bee, and so with the faith of a little child, who thinks everything will work out, I started working towards achieving my dream of being a teacher and author (and a whole host of other things).

It took many years (over a decade), but eventually I achieved my dream, and in the process, discovered that becoming an adult is not the goal of life. Biology ensures you will become an adult, if you live enough years. Success is not just growing old. Think of all the grown-ups you know and consider if they're happy, successful, flourishing, or if they're just cogs in the machine, miserable and unhappy. When was the last time you saw a happy adult on TV? They're rare, especially if you watch the news. Most adults are unhappy because hidden in the lesson to "be an adult" is the command to "exterminate" one's inner child. Yet, it's this inner child that looks upon the world with wonder and excitement, both of which motivate us to have fun, even when doing hard work. In fact, it's our inner child that first imagined the fantastic person you were to become and the future existence you're supposed to be living. If you get rid of your inner child, then you're destroying the being who originally dreamed the dream of your future happiness. So, it makes no sense to cut oneself off from one's inner child, just to become an adult whose happiness is defined by the trappings of other miserable adults. In this episode I'm going to get a little philosophical and suggest that the goal of life is to be reborn as an adult who has learned how to let their inner child-self shine through their existence. Stated less poetically, you must find a way to combine the wisdom and knowledge of being an adult with the wonder and excitement of a child engaged in creating and living a life worthy of living.

I'VE SPENT MOST OF MY LIFE in some sort of spaceship. It started as a child under my grandparents' kitchen table. I would push in all of the seats, climb underneath the table, then spend what seemed like hours firing thrusters, contacting aliens, and doing whatever else came to my imagination. (I still have the old table, and though I can't fit underneath it anymore, I've told my three-year-old son that our table is really a spaceship.) My other spaceships include my truck, my bike, and anywhere else I find myself alone with my imagination. I have a shirt that says, "I might look like I'm listening, but I'm really listening to KISS in my head." Well, I'm just as likely to be off on some space adventure, instead of paying attention to the world around me.

This approach to life reminds me a lot of acting. Acting requires a balance (one that's often overlapping) between making oneself open and vulnerable, while at the same time hiding one's true feelings. Life is much the same way. We have this inner self, often the same fragile child who became a teen, struggling to navigate between what we want others to see and what others actually see. Take, for instance, Tom's first marriage. Though I'm sure there was something they saw in each other, it appears to have been a relationship where both were playing roles without ever showing their true selves. Once Tom let his inner feelings show, he was kicked out and abandoned.

Sometimes dramatic breakups are the best thing for an individual, for they promote self-examination and motivate us to follow our deepest dreams. Here's an example of what I mean from my life. Around the time I turned 19, shortly after moving back home after a failed attempt at college, I got tired of my mother's attitude—I just wanted to be left alone. So after her giving me a list of chores one morning, I packed all my belongings into the back of my truck, wrote a check for the money I owed her, and drove away into the sunset. It wasn't as romantic as I make it sound. I gave her the check and said I was leaving, she was shocked and questioned my motives, and I got into my truck, drove away, and tried to figure out where I was going to sleep. I would spend the next few months homeless, living out of the back of my truck. I continued to work, often bathing in the dishwasher sinks before anyone else arrived (the sinks were never used, so I violated no health and safety standards), and would sleep in the woods, parking lots, or sometimes at a friend's house. I enjoyed my free time hiking, reading philosophy and Goethe's *The Sorrows of Young Werther*, and traveling. It was one of the best and most liberating times of my life, and it was all because the tension between me and my mother forced my inner self to take charge and follow my dreams. No, my dream was not to be homeless, but being homeless took me closer to my dream of being a teacher and author than staying at my mother's house, playing video games, and listening to music all day.

Back to acting, I know that Shakespeare and Rush declared "all the world's a stage," and to a large extent they are both correct. For example, there's a moment before you go on stage where you must decide whether you let your inner self remain hidden or if you're going to drop your defenses and let it shine through your performance. I've seen many actors fail, including myself, at this one crucial moment, just as I've seen adults fail at living their lives. In both instances, they refuse to drop their defenses and shine. Don't misunderstand me. I'm not describing people who hold ignorant racist and bigoted views finally deciding they're going to let the world know they are ignorant, racist, and bigoted. I'm talking about letting your inner child—that small kid who once discovered the world for the first time, who developed hopes and dreams about the future—rise to the surface of your being. Releasing your inner self requires you let go of the trappings of becoming an adult, which tell you to forget the imagination, forget creativity, forget fun.

Instead, releasing your inner self challenges you to become the creative force you once envisioned for the future.

Acting doesn't mean you are simply pretending to be someone else. When you were a child, whether you remember it or not, you were constantly trying on new character traits in order to decide what you liked and disliked. This process continues into adolescence and even adulthood, though it often becomes less pronounced as you get older. By experimenting with different character traits, we become a person—the word 'person' originates from 'personae', the character an individual exhibits. Through these character traits we find the self we like best and live our life accordingly, though sometimes external forces (significant others, friends, bosses, colleagues, etc.) will often attempt to decide who we become. For Tom, he used the Doctor as a cover for his "smallness of mind and [...] lack of real courage." Before long, the personae of the Doctor became the person of Tom Baker. He worked hard to ensure no one ever wanted to see or know the real Tom Baker, and to a large extent, he has been successful. Some might read this and find themselves skeptical: I'm supposed to act like someone else, hiding the real me, while at the same time letting the real me shine? For the most part, the answer to the question is "yes." We sometimes mistakenly believe our self is fully formed from the moment we're born, then develops slightly as we get older. While it's true that children are born with certain dispositions, the character of their self develops over a lifetime. We learn from the adults who raise us, from our friends, and from our communities (including the popular culture). The process of becoming an adolescent and eventually an adult is a constant process of us "trying on" different personality types and character traits. I went through phases where I pretended to be the Doctor, then MacGyver, then my grandfather, then Jerry Lewis, then David Lee Roth, and so on. We all do it, whether we're aware of it or want to admit it.

As we get older, it becomes harder to try on new personalities, yet it can still happen. *Doctor Who* (and other) conventions give us spaces in which we can try on new personalities, as do going to college, moving, vacations, and of course, major life events. Is it easy? No. In fact, as you get older, it's more akin to a Cyberman being graceful. As Tom notes, he once tried to convince the showrunners of *Doctor Who* to write a script where the Cybermen watched videos of Fred Astaire and Ginger Rogers (two famous dancers/actors) so they could learn to be less stiff and more graceful. They just laughed at his idea. The good news for us is that often we only need to convince ourselves. Yes, if you start speaking with a British accent to life-long friends, they might laugh and question your motives, but that's something you should expect. I imagine, if speaking with a British accent is part of your life goals, then your friends won't be too surprised. What I'm suggesting is more nuanced than changing our accents: you might say, "I'm going to be more (or maybe, less) adventurous," "I'm going to be more honest," "I'm going to do the opposite of what the voice in my head tells me," or maybe, "I'm going to do more of what the voice in my head is telling me to do." You begin with gradual changes, which then lead to greater changes, learning to do a few things that make you uncomfortable from time to time. This is how we, as adults, rediscover and let our inner child shine.

LIFE AS AN ADULT IS SOMETIMES terrifying. You never know if you're doing it "right," and no matter how many books you read or gurus you consult, as the credits begin to roll at the end of your life, you're the only one responsible for how you lived. One minute you're the star of the greatest television series ever, then next, as Tom describes his experience of leaving *Doctor Who* and getting a haircut, no one recognizes you. Not being recognized, however, can be a good thing, especially if you're seeking change.

Much of the happiness of life depends on taking calculated risks based on honest personal motives, and how we interpret the experiences that result. I chose *Doctor Who* and music as an escape from the drudgery of being a teen. Many thought I was wasting my time, especially when I would choose *Doctor Who* and music over my college work. At the time, I probably should've stopped going to college, but as an eighteen-year-old I still felt beholden to my mother to go. By my mid-twenties I had learned how to manage time and was ready for college. I learned how to infuse my two loves with my educational pursuits, eventually making all three part of my career. I simply had to translate the many hours spent "wasted" on *Doctor Who* and music into research for the work in which I dedicated my life.

The same is true for relationships—no matter what happens we must find a way to translate events in ways that help us cope and flourish. Tom talks of how getting married helped him avoid the terrors of real life. The flaw in his reasoning became apparent as he discovered that his heart was more concerned with going to the pub with friends than developing a marriage. I, too, was married for a brief period. Coming from a broken home, I was fascinated by marriage and wanted to be the first in my sibling group to show how a marriage could be successful. So, as a 19-year-old, I jumped at the opportunity to get married. At the time, I felt as though I was in love, and getting married promised an escape from North Mississippi to New Orleans. Looking back, the marriage was more for convenience than anything else. I wanted to get out of Tupelo, she wanted to get away from her home. We shared interests in cooking, but that fell apart, and instead of New Orleans, we settled on Hattiesburg, MS. We came from two completely different backgrounds, and instead of finding a compromise, we began living separate lives. Within four years, we were divorced. I immediately thought: FAILURE. Yet, as I began to make sense of the situation, I consciously decided to interpret my role differently, as a SURVIVOR—cue Destiny's Child.

Don't get me wrong, the event was a disaster, but it allowed me the chance to self-reflect on what was important in my life, and it motivated me to take control. Hopefully, I would never *not* recognize her, as Tom failed to recognize one of his ex-wives. If anything, if I saw her, I would thank her for being wise enough to openly question why we were together, which was the event that led to our separation and divorce. It was during this time that I both changed my college major back to my original love, philosophy, and began the slow process of becoming an author. Both changes were difficult, but I started small and continually worked on bettering myself. One of the hardest things to do was to create quiet times when I would simply jot down ideas and/or read (and try to understand) something new. Both of these habits took many years to develop, but I was so successful that I now have to schedule "noisy time" in order to watch TV or play video games.

With my life slowly moving in the direction for which I dreamed, the world offered many new adventures. I made new friends, including my mother. I've heard about other people who were friends with their parents, but I had never experienced such a relationship, except for a brief few years in the early 2000s. Sadly, it wouldn't last—parents will be parents. I also made a lot of new friends as I attempted to return to school. I was typically the oldest one in the class, but before long, I met several people who filled my life with many wonderful experiences. I'll talk more about work in the next section, but one of the greatest things to happen during this time period was that I quit my stable, well-paying job. Normally, such an event would be a bad thing, but devastating breakups are also wonderful opportunities for change.

What made this change of jobs so important was that it allowed me to see how limited my professional opportunities were and to meet my future wife. In regard to the former, I saw my leaving as an opportunity to get out of the restaurant business, but my only experience was in restaurants. No one else wanted me, which made me realize the severity of my situation: if I don't change who I am now, I will never become who I want to be. With no other options, out of money and depending on payday loans to cover rent, I walked into a competing restaurant and was hired on the spot. I would've never guessed, but my decision to walk into the Hattiesburg, MS Chili's that afternoon would soon introduce me to my future wife and life-partner, Jenny. She was dating someone when we first met, but with my charm, and references from co-workers that I wasn't a serial killer, she would eventually go with me on a date. Let me explain:

In 2001, I was a longhaired, goatee-, bandana-, and tie-dyed-wearing Deadhead who looked like a biker. Jenny was a quiet, sweet, loveable person who looked like she would never be caught dead with the likes of me. She would stand across from the kitchen area ensuring her orders were correct and being prepared in a timely fashion. As a result, I started asking her to bring me Arnold Palmers (sweet tea and lemonade). One evening while we were closing, the salad station guy and I were flirting with her. I wrote out my number and vital information, and offered it to her as an "application." My hope was that she would be so charmed and flattered that she'd go out with me that evening. That's not exactly what happened. She giggled and went about her closing duties, and I found out the next day that she was already dating someone in the restaurant—doh! I never flirted with her again, though I still asked for my Arnold Palmers.

A few months later, one of our co-workers invited me to a group outing, and to my surprise, Jenny was there—by herself. As the evening continued, after some great Italian food and several glasses of Chianti, I discovered she was single. With as much game as I could muster, I said (in a low, Barry-White-like voice) as she parted, "I know you just got out of a relationship, and I don't want to pressure you, but if you want to go out on a date sometime, I would like that." Were those the exact words? You'd have to ask her, but this is my story, and that's what I remember. Regardless, she said yes, checked with a co-worker to ensure I was "safe," and we had a date.

Our first date was February 12, 2002, and I know people warn about not starting a relationship so close to Valentine's Day, but it was the best decision of my life. I was so excited I didn't even know the date until later, and to this day we celebrate our first date instead of Valentine's. We started having quick dates, like blueberry pancakes at IHOP or kite flying and disc golf in the afternoon. I often joke that she introduced me to her parents on our second date, but it was more like the fourth—she was so hooked. I was too, but wanted to take it slow, which is the best approach I would advise for young couples—take your time. We had a two-year romance where we learned about each other, carefully approaching the relationship with the proper motives and expectations. The beginning phase of our relationship culminated in a trip to New Orleans to get engaged, marriage on her grandparents' tree farm in Big Level, MS, on May 15, 2006, and over sixteen years of loving friendship.

BESIDE RELATIONSHIPS, JOBS OFFER THE most enjoyment and/or stress in our life. In one way, jobs provide our identity: ask someone what they do, and more than likely, they will talk about where they work. In other ways, jobs protect us from reality, keeping us from exploring our identity and the challenges of life outside of our sphere or work. I've already mentioned how leaving my secure, well-paying job was scary, but it allowed me to more easily live the life I wanted. Staying at my old job was too easy: I could depend on it to "protect" me from failing at life. If you need an example, I knew countless people in the restaurant business who talked of trips to Europe, quitting, and all sorts of other things, and they never achieved any of their goals. They just kept showing up to work. I don't mean they were inferior or should be pitied. We all struggle with the tension between our dreams and reality. I just want to say that often the reason we don't achieve our dreams is because we choose not to fight for them, while other times we find ourselves in a place where we don't know how to proceed.

Tom's life is no different. He left *Doctor Who* for the great unknown, and as you might suspect he had his successes and failures. As an actor he was typecast, and as an individual, he had so intertwined the personae of the Doctor with Tom Baker, that it made others hesitant to cast him in non-Doctor-type roles. For instance, one of the interesting aspects of his role as Sherlock Holmes was that instead of playing him like the Doctor, who is a type of Sherlock Holmes character, he played him strait-laced. It didn't help that it was *The Hounds of Baskerville*, which features Watson more than Holmes, but even as a viewer, it's hard not to see Tom as the Doctor trying to be strait-laced. What's comforting about Tom's life story is, like us, he shows readers and viewers that we all must make difficult decisions throughout our lives. Just because we're a beloved Time Lord, doesn't mean we don't have to risk comfort for the possibility of something greater. Even after *Doctor Who*, Tom left a secure and fun job touring with the Royal Shakespeare Company for a film that never worked out. Did he give up? No. He simply went on with his life making what he took to be the best choices that would bring him the most happiness. He found roles in movies and television, and eventually, he would star as the narrator of shows like *Little Britain* and participate in the highly successful Big Finish series of *Doctor Who* audio adventures.

As an adult, especially with the advent of the Internet, Tom remained a steady part of my life. As a teen, I would often come home from working ten-hour-shifts in a restaurant and find comfort watching one of the Fourth Doctor's adventures. I once left the restaurant business for a short period, selling environmental cleaning systems (a fancy phrase for vacuum cleaners). I left the vacuum cleaner business to work on a farm, until the owner put me to work in his foam factory. Again, I found solace in Tom. I returned to restaurants, and even in the midst of the pain and turmoil of slowly giving my life away to them, watching the opening credits of Tom's *Doctor Who* stories transported me away into a place where life was bearable. Like the ever-present sound of music when visiting New Orleans, Tom became a part of my existence, and though he was often used to escape a life of meaningless work, something more was occurring as a result of our relationship.

As Aristotle notes, true friendship is a relationship where each person benefits from the flourishing of the other. We delight in spending time with and helping our true friends, as do they; and so together, true friends help each other grow and flourish. Though I have no idea what my life gives to or if my life in anyway benefits Tom, Tom is an ever-present influence. When I was a teen I thought I was simply using Tom as an escape, but as he continued to live out his life, I realized he was actually helping develop aspects of myself that I had no idea were in need of developing. Because Tom wrote an autobiography, I did something I never under normal circumstances would do: I turned off the TV and music, sat, and read a book. I read and enjoyed a book! Fast forward twenty years to 2020, and I read a couple books every week, but in 2000, I was too busy for books. Tom inspired me to read on a regular basis, which prepared me for being successful in college. The stories he told, with all of their honesty, awkwardness, and freedom, inspired me to live an inspired life worthy of being retold. (At least I think it's worthy of being retold.) Therefore, I credit Tom with planting the seeds that would eventually lead me from restaurants into the classroom, and also behind a computer where I would learn to write my own stories.

You never know where life will lead. By 2001, I dedicated my life to finishing school. I started by taking some classes at Jones County Junior College, where friends and mentors (recall the lesson from Episode Two) helped me stay on the right path. Next, I returned to the University of Southern Mississippi (USM), officially re-declaring my major in Philosophy. As I was having success in school, I met my future wife, graduated, and after gaining my Master's degree from USM, moved to Knoxville, TN to work on my Doctorate at the University of Tennessee. You see, because my friend Tom was the Doctor, I knew I needed to be a doctor too. Graduate school was full of challenges, but as Tom never gave up, I decided I wouldn't either. Some in my department at the University of Tennessee tried to convince me to quit, because they thought I was more of a historian and would never be a "successful" philosopher, but I refused to listen and kept following my dream. I received my PhD in 2012, and after spending a year at the University of Alabama at Birmingham, settled down in Owensboro, KY, at Owensboro Community and Technical College.

Throughout all of these transitions, I worked to be brilliant, whether through success or failure, just as Tom showed me was possible. One thing I noticed was that I was successful when I worked with others to help achieve my dreams and to help them achieve theirs; whereas, failure tended to occur when I tried to go off by myself and do it alone. In fact, all of my failures are the result of me losing sight of what's important in my life, attempting to live up to the expectations of others. My successes occur when I think long and hard about the child that's within me. Is what I'm doing worthy of the child within? Would he be excited and proud, or skeptical and ashamed? Do my dreams still match his? To be honest with oneself is sometimes the hardest thing in life, but I've learned (am still learning) that if our adult self is incompatible with our child self, then we will never flourish. Granted, there are some who have had traumatic childhoods, but even with tragedy, I imagine there's a small voice of hope and joy worthy of co-existence. My childhood had its own turmoil, many things I chose not to mention, but I've found that when I listen to the voice that is my child-self, the thing that finds wonder in everything, I flourish; and when I lose track of that voice and get lost in being an adult that's when I find myself miserable, often plagued by failure.

SPEAKING OF FAILURE, ONE OF the most difficult things I ever suffered is the process of finding out that Jenny and I can't have our own biological children. We started trying shortly after getting married, with no luck. After several years, we decided to seek medical advice. We received some cursory explanations, but never received a definite reason why we were unable to have kids. We eventually stopped the tests, since they were getting more and more expensive. We had decided early on that instead of spending money on our own desires we would strive to help others through adoption.

Why did I feel like a failure? Mainly because I wanted to be father. My biological father was mostly absent. If I was lucky, I might see him for a few hours during the summer, and even as I got older, he chose to remain aloof. I wanted to prove to myself I could be a father, and wanted to be there for a child who needed a father. Eventually, I realized the error in thinking myself a failure. Because of my absent father, I spent many years helping and mentoring children with several different organizations, including churches and Big Brothers Big Sisters. It was these sorts of activities that helped me realize how little biological connectedness matters in the grand scheme of things. I began to recognize all of the fathers I had growing up—men who took the time to talk and shepherd me through life. Then I recognized I had been doing the same. So, instead of defining myself a failure, I knew I had already been a father, and because Jenny and I embraced the idea of adoption we were prepared to be parents.

Adoption is no easy task. It takes about a year to fill out the paperwork, then you wait years for someone to pick you. During those years you receive many messages inquiring whether you're interested in a child from a particular situation—many situations are horrific, and due to confidentiality, I won't go into details; you'll just have to trust me when I say there are some women and children who exist in difficult situations that are beyond the imagination. As for us, we had some biological parents pick us to be in their top three, which meant we had to interview in hopes of being picked. Besides the waiting, such interviews were the most difficult. All you can do is be honest and hope they see something in you they like, but I tend to overanalyze things, so when we weren't picked, I would naturally find some reason to blame myself.

One day all the waiting and self-incrimination ended. Due to several factors, our adoption agent suggested that adoption might never happen. In Kentucky there were (are!) some lawyers who found ways to skirt the legal restrictions on adoptions, and they were (are!) selling babies for astronomical amounts of money. As a result, standard adoptions were more difficult, and so, there wasn't much hope for us to get a child. It was the holiday season, cold, and depressing, and there we were facing the possibility of never having a child. Then, all of the sudden, while drowning ourselves in pasta at Olive Garden, we received a phone call saying that a mother had picked us. We were excited! The mother was due in three days. We were scared!! Adoption is a rollercoaster, but we were ready; and after a couple of weeks (we found out that three days was a guess), we welcomed our son Elliott Storm into our lives: Elliott after my paternal grandfather, and Storm after a dear friend who passed away in a car accident—still miss you Brian, and wish we were still making movies and acting in plays. Thankfully, my job as a professor allows me to spend many hours with Elliott, and I have successfully made him a bigger *Doctor Who* fan than myself. Though he's only three, he loves the Fifth and Sixth Doctors the best (and seems to have a thing for Tegan after having met Janet Fielding at WHOlanta), and will spend all day watching the title sequences, if I would only let him.

It's hard not to write pages about Elliott, but I'll limit myself. He's all one could ever ask for in a child. He's full of energy, loves music, and in addition to *Doctor Who*, would be happy spending all day cuddling and pulling on my ear, (again) if I let him. He keeps me busy and wears me out, but every minute spent with him reminds me of what's important in life. To be honest, I didn't think I would be a good dad, but I decided early on to embrace the challenge with confidence and to see mistakes as opportunities for improvement. As a philosopher, I struggled with the onslaught of new emotions. I still do, but being a parent is a work in progress that I'm determined to master—or at least not die trying.

I should mention two more things before this episode comes to a close. First, while working on my PhD, I took a short break to co-edit *Doctor Who and Philosophy: Bigger on the Inside*. Knowing it would be a disaster if I tried to do alone, I used the wisdom of a child and asked my good friend and mentor, Dr. Paula Smithka, to help me edit the book. She's as wise and sharp as they come, and because of her, the volume is one of Open Court's best-selling popular culture and philosophy books, currently on its ninth edition. We would also co-edit *More Doctor Who and Philosophy: Regeneration Time* a few years later, and I would begin writing my own books, including the one you're holding, *The Real Meaning of Doctor Who*, and *Repentance and the Right to Forgiveness.*

Second, because working on *Doctor Who and Philosophy* prolonged my PhD by a year, I was passed over for a job at Pellissippi State Community College. I had been working there as an Adjunct Professor, we loved the area, and hoped to stay. However, other opportunities arose, and we flourished despite not getting the job. In fact, if I had gotten the job, I would have never met many of the wonderful friends I have in Birmingham, AL and Owensboro, KY, and more importantly, I would have never met Elliott. (Love that little fella!) With that said, while finishing work on this book, I was offered a position to return to Knoxville, TN and teach at Pellissippi State Community College. We will miss the wonderful people of Owensboro, especially those friends, colleagues, and bandmates who did so much for and with us: thank you. We are nevertheless excited to see where the next phase of our adventure takes us. Hopefully, we'll adopt again, write a few more books, paint a few pictures, watch Elliott grow into a man, and who knows, maybe I'll get to meet Tom Baker one of these days.

WELL, THAT'S THE STORY OF MY life with Tom Baker, so far. You might have noticed that as the book developed, there was less of Tom and more of me. That's how life and friendships go: we as individuals incorporate the lessons and values of our mentors and friends until they simply become a part of who we are as individuals. We cease to be two separate beings, and exist in each other, as the remnants of lessons, ideas, and loves of one another. In my chapter "We're Gathered to Remember," found in *Futurama and Philosophy*, I argue that this is the most rewarding means of achieving immortality. Names on buildings and streets are forgotten and changed; monuments, money, power, and fame are fleeting; and DNA doesn't ensure you'll ever be thought of again. Only by sharing our lives with friends, then having them share their lives with others do we ensure a part of us never ceases to exist. People might not remember our name, just as I don't expect anyone will remember my name after a few years; but the love, care, and compassion I share with others will continue to exist as it's passed on to others through their acts of love, care, and compassion. This transmission of self is the main lesson of the entire *Doctor Who* franchise, and it's a lesson I only recognized because of my life with Tom Baker.

The same lesson is what allows us to become an adult and be reborn as a child. Since we can't physically be reborn as a child, our only option is to reincorporate our inner child's psychology into our adult self. This means we must spend time reflecting on the hopes, dreams, and fears we had as a child, which opens us to the possibility of working towards recommitting ourselves to those dreams. It's a transformative process that requires continual practice, for the world wants you to be an old crotchety adult; but if you work at it, you'll find childlike ways to interpret the world, which will then provide the space where you can flourish as a child reborn.

A lot of life is simply about how you interpret what is thrown at you. As adults, we forget about the optimism we had as a child. Kids believe in magic: toys are alive, bunnies bring them candy, a tooth fairy pays good money for teeth, and an old man at the North Pole keeps track of their moral lives. Adults believe that the only things for certain are death and taxes. Once you succumb to this adult belief, your world no longer contains magic. Think of it this way: if you approach a task knowing you hate it and it's pointless, you're going to be miserable performing the task. When I worked in restaurants, there were certain jobs that were the worst; but it wasn't long before I realized it was my belief that "they were the worst" that made them so awful. Once I realized that if I approached such tasks with excitement, they weren't so bad. As a more recent example, I changed my computer password to "I hate passwords," and it didn't take long for me to recognize the anger that occurred each time I logged in. I changed my password to "I love Elliott," and now I'm overcome with happiness when I login. The login didn't change, but I changed how I interpreted the process.

Tom showed me that being an adult isn't enough. We must relearn how to become kids, with all of their knowledge and wisdom. So, no matter what life throws at you as an adult, and it will throw a lot, you can weather the storms as they pass. No matter the circumstance, whether it's divorce, addiction, family strife, career setbacks, or a graduate program telling you three times to quit "because you'll never make it," you must learn how to rediscover the childlike wonder that helps you persevere. Tom helped me learn these lessons, and they are lessons I try to help others learn too. They are lessons that help me get up in the morning and keep striving to succeed, even though the grumpy, achy adult in me says, "Stay in bed, it's not worth it, no one cares, the world is a mess, and it'd better-off without you." (I told you the world of an adult can be cruel.) When your adult-self tells you such things, you must either ignore, which kids are great at doing, or reinterpret such things as: "GET UP, this is the only life you have, you care, go find others that care, the world needs your help, and the world is less-special, -unique, and -fantastic without you." Go live your life. Smile a little more. Wear a long scarf. Bask in your imagination. Don't let the doubters win. Accept the Jelly Baby. And live a life worthy of the life your inner child deserves.

EPISODE FOUR
REFLECTIONS ON THE WORK OF TOM BAKER

I do not always see what others see. In fact, after attending countless panel discussions at a variety of *Doctor Who* and science fiction conventions, I have noticed that I often miss what others seem to take as obvious. For instance, I never knew I was supposed to hate Adric or Kamelion, until I started attending conventions. Sure, I knew Adric could sometimes do annoying things and Kamelion was not the most mobile animatronic device, but my imagination has the ability to see beyond what is presented to what is intended. Much of my ignorance is the result of being absorbed in the show, but it also helps that I didn't have access to magazines and books that reviewed the show and shaped fan perceptions. In other words, I never read that I was supposed to hate Adric and Kamelion, so when they appeared, I took them as any six-year-old would: another weird character on a weird sci-fi show. My viewing lens was not clouded by someone else's interpretation of the show, so I was able to interpret the show as I saw fit. As a result, I often find my perspective of episodes and characters differs from others.

I don't think this makes me a poor judge of *Doctor Who* and entertainment. In fact, I would argue it gives me a considerable advantage over some viewers. It gives me the ability to more-easily grasp the intentions of the production, to think abstractly about the characters and storylines, and to offer insights into how the lessons of a production should be incorporated into our lives. In the following examination of Tom Baker's work, I will offer my insights into each performance, suggesting what I think is important, problematic, and sometimes troubling. I hope my reviews offer a unique perspective, and that some of you will find a new voice for how to interpret certain episodes and characters.

DOCTOR WHO

Season 12

Robot (1974-1975)
Writer: Terrance Dicks
Script Editor: Robert Holmes
Director: Christopher Berry
Producer: Berry Letts

This is the serial where we get a new Doctor, he shows us his impressive amount of teeth, hair, and scarf, defeats a giant robot with some "soapy water," and begins the magic that will be Tom Baker and Lis Sladen. I didn't see this serial until after I had seen the rest of season 12, and several from Tom Baker's later seasons. Eventually I picked this up on VHS in the mid-1990s. My first thoughts were: that was fun, but a little strange looking. I had no knowledge of how it was filmed as part of season 11, with the previous Doctor's production team. All I cared about was that it was the Fourth Doctor's first story, it had Sarah Jane, and it featured a giant robot—three of my favorite things in life! There is not much depth to the story. It is your typical mad scientists taking over the world in the strangest way possible—let us blow up the world and then rebuild it. The easier thing to do would have been to use the disintegrator gun to simply go around and covertly get rid of everyone and everything that is causing the world to be so crummy. At least that's how I would do it!

Nevertheless, the serial is fun, with the Doctor and Sarah Jane exploding off the screen with great smiles and charisma. Granted, nothing compares to Tom's full-frontal nudity in *The Canterbury Tales*, but it is exciting nonetheless. Tom Baker commands every scene. If not for his overwhelming personality, he would come off as abusive; but as we will come to notice over the next few seasons, this is the Doctor's new personality: the all-wise, four steps ahead, and champing at the bit to show his cleverness and save the universe. The Doctor is quite different from his processors, and spends a lot of time lying down, and his attitude has definitely changed. He's more cavalier and not overly-concerned with the threat of nuclear annihilation or giant robots.

My biggest complaint is the introduction of Dr. Harry Sullivan. Even though there are episodes in which Sullivan shines as a character, he tends to frustrate and irritate me. He just doesn't add much to the show. I know he was brought on in case the producers hired an older Doctor, because they wanted to ensure some action, but even as an action star Sullivan is an odd choice. A better choice would have been Sgt. Benton, who had already established himself as capable. His reserved wit and compassion would have made a nice addition to the Doctor and Sarah Jane. What is more, as Benton shows in "Robot," he is also good at making a hot mug of tea! All things considered, it's a good story, a strong beginning to the Fourth Doctor's reign, and a nice sendoff for Barry Letts, Terrance Dicks, and the Third Doctor's production team.

The Ark in Space (1975)
Writer: Robert Holmes (John Lucarotti, uncredited)
Script Editor: Robert Holmes
Director: Rodney Bennett
Producer: Philip Hinchcliffe

Things get interesting, right about now. The Doctor and companions are on a seemingly vacant space station, with automated defenses, snobby-high-class future humans, bug-aliens, and the eerie atmosphere of *Doctor Who* that makes me love the show so much. Though I don't remember watching this episode on television, it seems so familiar (the space station, the greenness, etc.) that I'm sure I saw at least some of it when I was young.

With the first episode focusing on the TARDIS crew, the biggest threat is Harry Sullivan: he sends them off course, almost kills Sarah Jane, and continually attacks viewers with his antiquated thinking. Don't get me wrong, Ian Marter is a fine actor who is convincing as Harry Sullivan, but he is written as a buffoon. On one level it works, because it keeps the Doctor's abrasiveness from being off-putting. There are times when Harry is in his element and contributes nicely to episodes, but not in this one.

Back on topic: With his witty banter, determination, and cleverness, Tom Baker feels like he has been playing the Doctor for years. Couple his performance with the story, lighting, and direction, "The Ark in Space" is truly classic *Doctor Who*. Weird space aliens that resemble creepy bugs, converting anyone who touches them, a possessed, psychotic *übermensch*, and the human race on the brink—what else could you ask for from *Doctor Who*? Some people like to complain about the special effects, but such complaints miss the point. *Doctor Who* is about the imagination, and how with enough creativity and cleverness, we humans might just survive and thrive. Maybe my mind is on a different wavelength, but I don't see what others love to complain about. A friend once said that I was like one of Pavlov's dogs: every time *Doctor Who* comes on, my mind is transported to a happy dimension. I always liked that explanation, but more accurately, my imagination is able to see what the production teams were trying to create, without getting distracted in the real-life limitations of the show. As a result, I can enjoy the show, no matter how many people crawl around in sleeping bags, have bubble-wrapped hands, or how many times I see strings, mirrors, and wobbles. In my head, it's more real than the most advanced computer animation available today.

Though I feel like I saw this serial as a kid, without evidence, the best I can say is that I didn't see the serial until I purchased it on VHS in the early 1990s. Once purchased, however, it became a fast favorite. I would often show it to friends interested in *Doctor Who*, and it always made a fun watch after a long night working at a restaurant. There's really no bad place to start watching, and by the time you reach the end, you can't wait to see the next adventure. As a fun side note, after a day of enjoying the New Orleans Jazz and Heritage festival in 2004, as a bachelor party gift to myself, I upgraded to the DVD. What can I say? Love was in the air, and I decided it was time to make the plunge and convert my *Doctor Who* collection to DVD. Those of you who have struggled with whether or not to switch to DVD after spending countless dollars on VHS know that like marriage, such a commitment was significant. "The Ark in Space" was my first step in this long commitment. I would say, "I'm not doing it again," but thanks to the new Blu-ray releases, it looks like I'm again in the process of conversion.

The Sontaran Experiment (1975)
Writer: Bob Baker and Dave Martin
Script Editor: Robert Holmes
Director: Rodney Bennett
Producer: Philip Hinchcliffe

It was a cold, dark, and rainy night on September 17, 1983, when I sat down on the floor of my grandparents' house to watch what I would later learn was called "The Sontaran Experiment." To be honest, I have no idea what the weather was. Being in Mississippi, it was probably hot and muggy. All I know for certain is that this is the first episode I fully remember watching as a young six-year-old boy. What does that mean? It means this was the first time I saw Tom Baker, Lis Sladen, a Sontaran, and the sonic screwdriver. No TARDIS in the episode, but the time ring was cool enough for me. It made the introduction of the TARDIS in later episodes even more exciting! I never noticed it wasn't Tom Baker in most of the scenes, or that the robot was some flimsy piece of junk on wheels—I just assumed it was flying.

As I look back on the serial, what I like most is the location. The dreariness of it all, the rain slickers, the crevasses, and the myriad tunnels created a landscape that allowed for hours of imaginative fun on my own. I, now, realize that much of the movement was a practical necessity of *Doctor Who* (and many other shows), where they would make sets feel more expansive by having them move around and go through the same corridors in different directions. I played in the same way: one tree could be a ship, a base, a cell, and who knows what else? Little did I know that the same imaginative play was the foundation of much of television! When I directed my short film *The Meaning of Life* (https://youtu.be/MfKK1VkoDA8), I made sure to use the same technique.

I still enjoy the serial, even though knowing that Tom isn't in many of the scenes makes it a little more difficult to enjoy. The rest of the story and the actors deliver the goods. I don't say it often, but Harry Sullivan is fantastic! He has wit, serves a purpose, and is competent at getting the job done. If only he were just as strong in other serials. Tom Baker is still witty, clever, and capable of defeating the Sontarans. And what a way to defeat them: bluff them out of invading a completely empty planet! It's a good thing the Sontarans didn't have the technology to detect life-signs. And speaking of clever, I still love the idea that humans abandoned Earth, were divided by class strife, and somehow randomly arrive back at Earth at the right time. Not only that, but they are going to have to work together to repopulate the Earth. It's just a fun serial helped by the fact there are only two episodes. Anything longer would have been disastrous. Tom and the crew get in, save the day, and transmat off to a new adventure.

Another nice aspect of the show is how it created an extended story arc. As viewers, we see them arrive via transmat, and when they leave, we expect them to return to Nerva Beacon. Instead, as seen in the next episode, they get conscripted to do some dirty work for the Time Lords, then work their way back to Nerva Beacon. The writers do a nice job removing the TARDIS from the storyline and creating a nice feel of connection between episodes. In fact, these serials have a stronger internal consistency than some of the later attempts to create season long story arcs (e.g. The Key to Time). There were hints of this approach in the Pertwee years, and the New Series has mastered the season-long story arc, but Season 12 feels like it could pass as part of the New Series. Of course, Season 12 does not have the big season-ending climax like we would get in the New Series, but it is a fun season that keeps you coming back week to week, or in Blu-ray-DVD terms, hitting "Play All."

Genesis of the Daleks (1975)
Writer: Terry Nation
Script Editor: Robert Holmes
Director: David Maloney
Producer: Philip Hinchcliffe

Bring on the Daleks! Not only was this a seminal serial in my childhood, but it's the serial that inspired the book you're holding. I like to imagine that my experience of the Daleks mirrored the experience of those children who saw their first appearance in "The Daleks" (1963-64). I was terrified and amazed at the same time. I was too young to understand the Nazi references, to care about man-eating clams, and I seriously doubt I sat through the entire two-and-a-half-hour broadcast—I was six, and had strict rules of teeth-brushing and bedtime.

What I do remember, however, are two scenes that remain powerful reminders of the greatness of the serial and the nature of good vs. evil. First, the Doctor's dialogue with Davros over whether Davros would condone the use of a contagion capable of destroying all life. Not only would Davros condone its use, but he imagines holding a capsule of the contagion and breaking it with the tiny pressure of his fingers. What an insanely good scene. Not only would he use the contagion, but he would crush it himself, thereby killing himself and everything else! What power, what control, what insanity?! Tom Baker's delivery and execution of this scene is masterful. He's been tortured, forced to reveal the future of the Daleks, and is still capable to wax philosophically about morality and ethics. It turns out to be a rouse, and the Doctor attempts to force Davros to destroy the Daleks. Eventually, Tom figures out a way to escape, but this scene opened my mind to science, ethics, evil, and good writing and acting. When I started teaching Ethics, I would use the scene as a discussion starter, challenging students to answer the Doctor's question and respond to Davros's reply.

The second scene is where the Doctor argues with Sarah Jane over whether or not to EXTERMINATE the little Dalek "hatchlings." Tom could have played the scene in any number of ways, but he chose to interact with Sarah Jane as an equal, genuinely concerned and interested with what she thought. Similar to the first, the scene touches on several ethical issues, including the major ethical divide between consequentialism (consequences determine when an action is right) and non-consequentialism (consequences are irrelevant). Of course, I didn't understand such conceptual issues in 1983, but I did notice that this was a serious issue, one that had me asking: "Could I kill a child, even if I knew s/he would later become evil?" I know some people tend to think children incapable of understanding complex ideas and principles, but I'm not one of them. Children are smart, resourceful, and capable of understanding all sorts of concepts and theories—especially if they have adults willing to answer questions and explain ideas. I had a mother and two brothers who weren't afraid to answer questions, and I had Tom Baker willing to both ask questions and live out their answers. These scenes set the paradigm—the interpretive framework—for which I would understand (and still do understand) *Doctor Who*, and to a large extent, life.

I've already talked about how Tom Baker was great in the episode, but to be honest, everyone was at the top of their respective games. Elisabeth Sladen and Ian Marter were spot-on. Whether in the thick of things, or running back and forth between Thal and Kaled domes, they added excitement and energy to a fairly lengthy serial. Michael Wisher's Davros still captivates, Peter Miles's Nyder was a perfectly devious companion to Davros, and Guy Siner, my favorite actor from *'Allo! 'Allo!*, makes a special appearance as Ravon—I wonder if he knows the location of the sausage containing "The Fallen Madonna with the Big Boobies"? (Sorry, it's not often I get to make *'Allo! 'Allo!* references!) Besides the occasional Sullivan-eating clam, I really have no complaints. Loved the Guardian, the proto-Daleks, and the general suspense felt throughout the show. The sets were well-lit and engaging, the pacing was good, and the extras and guest stars felt convincing—Harriet Philpin's Bettan could've easily joined the TARDIS crew. It kind of makes me sad to think of her eventual fate at the hands of the Daleks, but maybe she found a way to escape.

One final note, when released on VHS, "Genesis" was paired with "The Sontaran Experiment" as a two VHS set. What a great deal! The only problem I had was that my VHS of "Genesis" lacked the first two episodes. It started with Sarah Jane dropping from the scaffolding. I found this odd, but due to my knowledge of missing episodes, I assumed these were just two of the causalities. This was the case until I received a copy of "Genesis" with the "missing" first two episodes. A mystery! So, I began pondering why my VHS copy would be missing two episodes, and then it dawned on me: 1) most VHS tapes would hold two hours of material at a standard speed; 2) there is a total of six episodes for "Genesis," which equal about 140 minutes, with only four episodes on the second VHS totaling, 90 minutes; 3) "The Sontaran Experiment" is only two episodes long (approximately 45 minutes)—Ding! Ding! Ding! There is room for the two "missing" episodes of "Genesis" after "The Sontaran Experiment." With this revelation, I called my brother Philip, who I'd given my VHS copy, and asked him to see if there were any episodes after "The Sontaran Experiment" on the first VHS. He didn't even have to look. He said, "Yeah, it's the first episode of "Genesis" [...:dummy]." He didn't actually say "dummy," but I could hear it in his voice. How could I have missed it? I don't know, but it still give me a chuckle: the hours lamenting these poor lost episodes, when they were in my collection the whole time. Makes me hope that one day we'll find all of the missing *Doctor Who* episodes setting in the BBC vault, possibly labeled as "The Sontaran Experiment!"

Revenge of the Cybermen (1975)
Writer: Gerry Davis (Robert Holmes, uncredited)
Script Editor: Robert Holmes
Director: Michael E. Briant
Producer: Philip Hinchcliffe

I catch a lot of flak over this one, but if loving "Revenge of the Cybermen" is wrong, then cover me in gold dust and send me to Voga. I've watched (and re-watched) this serial more than any other, and continue to watch it on a regular basis. I first saw it on October 1, 1983, and there was something about the combination of a virus-infecting Cybermat, a space station, cave-dwelling aliens, and giant Cybermen that instantly blew my mind. This (with "The Brain of Morbius" coming in at a close second) was the serial that made me fall in love with Tom Baker and *Doctor Who*. There's a lot in this serial, so let's get to it.

First off, it begins with a nice discussion of timey-wimey stuff—Where's the TARDIS? Who knows? It might be traveling forward, or maybe backwards, to catch up with us! What a glorious concept for a six-year-old. It's one thing to think of traveling around in time, but to have events headed towards you from different temporal directions is a whole other story. Gotta say, I still enjoy pondering such possibilities. I also loved the whole "plague" story. Always found the notion of quarantine terrifying, especially when contracting the illness is only a matter of time. Add to the plague a creepy Cybermat who's actually the culprit of death, and you have one heck of a mystery. The final element is the villain "Kellman." Knowing the villain, and having the villain be so "hateable" (Joffrey-esque in his likeability), creates an intensity that is still felt to this day. Sure, there are issues with the story, especially with Kellman—in the end he's portrayed as a "good" guy, but there's no redemption. To construct such a convoluted plan that causes the death of so many innocent people makes him seem more a dangerous idiot than an evil genius. Nevertheless, there's an intense creepiness to the serial that makes it one of my favorite serials of all time.

For a fan of Tom Baker, there may be no better example of his charisma as the Doctor. From the moment the serial beings, Tom Baker is making discoveries, drawing conclusions about the nature of the space station, fixing transmats, reprograming Cybermats, and "dying"— what a great cliffhanger! Tom's fascination with the Cybermen is palpable. He's curious and irreverent at the same time. He gets his shoulders crushed, smiles, passes out, then critiques the Cybermen for their rubbish English—"'Fragmatized'? I don't suppose we can expect decent English from a machine." Tom is natural, intense, and at his best; and if you listen closely while the Doctor holds the Cyberbomb and threatens to "fragmatize" them all, there's even a nice Pink Floyd sound effect from "Time" ticking away in the background. I guess they only thought it fair, since Pink Floyd seems to have borrowed a melody from the *Doctor Who* theme on "One of These Days."

There are some drawbacks to the episode, and one of them is how the Doctor treats Harry Sullivan. I mentioned previously how I wasn't a big Sullivan fan, but "Revenge" actually allows him to play to his strengths as a physician.

He ends up playing second fiddle to the Doctor, but he does a nice job in the serial. It's not his fault the door slid open—as if leaning on it would slow it down. He didn't know that removing the harness would cause an explosion, and being called an "imbecile" is a little rough. To see the Doctor treat him so harshly detracts from an otherwise perfect performance from Tom.

The next big issue is that the corpses are a little "stiff." In fact, they're obviously mannequins! To be honest, I don't remember noticing them until fairly recently. I might have noticed them years ago and blocked the memory out, but when re-watching it with my two-year-old son in January 2019, I was no longer able to maintain the delusion. The problem is that it's hard to maintain the suspension of disbelief when you feel like the characters are walking through a department store after an earthquake. Stuffed dummies would've looked better, or maybe an explanation that the plague causes a unique type of rigor mortis. Anything would've been better than the choice to fill the set with dummies. Alas, I guess that's part of the charm of the show, even when the BBC is loaded with cash for *Doctor Who*—on the 2012 DVD cover of "Nightmare of Eden" you can see the faces of people inside the creatures' mouths. Some people cringe and avoid Classic Who for these reasons, but I find the budget constraints endearing. They never inhibit my enjoyment of an episode.

Besides these two complaints, "Revenge" is wonderful. I still remember making Ro*tel dip with my brothers, seeing who could add the most cayenne pepper, without getting up from the couch. With this hot-spicy-goodness, I fell in love with *my* Doctor. As for the serial, I love the mystery and subplots, the caves, civil war, bombs on backs, and little watercrafts. I don't even mind the make-up of the Vogans. I wouldn't want to be an actor in one of those facemasks, but I like the stiff effect—it reminds me of rock, which works because they live in caves. The supporting cast does a great job. With minimal screen time, they are still able to illicit empathy for their characters. I'm genuinely sad to see the crew suffer and die, except for Kellman. Most surprisingly (at least for me), after re-watching Tom's first season as the Doctor, I must admit that Harry Sullivan has grown on me. I still struggle during his first two serials, and some of his phrasing, like "ol' girl," is off-putting, but when he's allowed to be a doctor and he's less condescending, he makes a good companion, especially with some of his interactions with Sarah Jane. I've come to realize he does a large amount of great work in several episodes, but when he's annoying, he *is* annoying. To top-off the serial and the season, the ol' girl, I mean TARDIS, returns—sorry, I guess Sullivan is rubbing off on me. What a way to end the season and to set up what would be some of the best years of *Doctor Who* and television.

Season 12 Summation

Season 12 is a strong season, arguably the best of Tom Baker's tenure on *Doctor Who*. It's definitely one of my favorites, with only a few detractions. Seasons 13 and 14 are so good that they might win in head-to-head combat, but there are days 12 might come out on top. I would rank the episodes in the following way. As previously noted, "Revenge of the Cybermen" is my favorite, but I realize that my love of the serial is more sentimental than based on hard evidence. So, with my love of "Revenge of the Cybermen" stated, "The Sontaran Experiment" comes in at number five. It's a good story, and I like the two episode format, but the lack of Tom Baker due to his broken collarbone causes it to come in last. "Robot" ranks fourth and "Revenge of the Cybermen" third. Even with the apparent shortcomings of the latter, the eeriness of "Revenge of the Cybermen" and the return of the Cybermen make it superior to "Robot." "The Ark in Space," with the proper introduction of Philip Hinchcliffe's production team, makes it one of Tom's greats—regardless of the bubble wrap and clunky insect costumes. That leaves "Genesis of the Daleks" as number one. With its epic reintroduction of the Daleks, compelling storyline, and overall direction (minus the clams), it's hard to imagine any other serial from Season 12 as superior to "Genesis." R. Alan Siler, author of *Children of Time: The Companions of* Doctor Who and Doctor Who*'s Greatest Hits*, correctly sums it up saying, "[It's] a topnotch story that makes the Daleks real and threatening… [an] incredibly iconic story with scenes that defined Baker's Doctor…"

Season 12 Ranking

1. Genesis of the Daleks
2. The Ark in Space
3. Revenge of the Cybermen
4. Robot
5. The Sontaran Experiment

Season 13

Terror of the Zygons (1975)
Writer: Robert Banks Stewart
Script Editor: Robert Holmes
Director: Douglas Camfield
Producer: Philip Hinchcliffe

I remember watching "Terror of the Zygons" and being both scared and fascinated. I want to say this was the serial where my brothers and I were supposed to work out, but instead of working out, I made a milkshake and watched *Doctor Who*—I was always the wise one out of us three! The serial appeared on October 8, 1983, in Tupelo, MS, and it fit the fall mood perfectly. With aliens in disguise, my introduction to all things Scottish, and my favorite, Nessie the Loch Ness Monster, "Terror" was and remains one of my favorite stories.

The serial has a good pace, and there is a relaxed feeling to the whole affair that invites viewers to set back and be entertained. Ian is good, Sarah is fun, and their banter with the Doctor and the Brigadier creates a sense of family. Without knowing it at the time, it was a good send off for the Brigadier, giving him the opportunity to show off his legs and clan heritage. The serial has several innovative features, such as psycho crystals, squid-sucker controls, and the idea that the Loch Ness Monster is under the control of aliens. The Zygons come off as legitimate enemies, with their sweet whispering and human disguises. Of course, their effectiveness wouldn't be fully realized until their return in the 50th Anniversary Special in 2013, but they are still fun to watch in this story. Camfield's direction is nice. He creates a sense of fear with creepy angles, edge-of-your-seat episode-ending cliffhangers, mystic Scotsmen, spying deer heads, and aliens disguised as humans. The Doctor received another near-deadly backrub from the Zygons, but he also shows up in a Scottish tartan, letting his companions wear his normal garb. With all of this in mind, "Terror of the Zygons" sets the tone for the entire season, which is filled with so much greatness.

Holmes and Hinchcliffe hit their stride creating some of the greatest television ever made, cementing *Doctor Who* as one of the greatest sci-fi shows in history. They introduce gothic elements into the show, but still allow it to entertain features of its previous greatness, as witnessed under the direction of Barry Letts and Terrance Dicks. In fact, Letts directs a serial later in the season—"The Android Invasion." Tom flourishes in this creative environment, and any hesitation or uncertainty of the previous season is gone. He's in command, and whether the result of direction or his own playfulness, he comes into his own as the Doctor. In fact, by Season 13, it's difficult to tell where Tom ends and the Doctor begins. He has become the Doctor, and though we say goodbye to Harry Sullivan and Brigadier Lethbridge-Stewart in the serial, they remain part of the atmosphere of *Doctor Who*, and it is this atmosphere that makes watching Tom and *Doctor Who* such a unique and enjoyable experience.

Planet of Evil (1975)
Writer: Louis Marks
Script Editor: Robert Holmes
Director: David Maloney
Producer: Philip Hinchcliffe

For some reason I missed "Planet of Evil" when it aired on October 15, 1983. If I saw it, I don't remember. I first remember watching it in late 90s, when I received a glorious box of VHS tapes containing almost every Third, Fourth and Fifth Doctor serial recorded from New Hampshire Public Television. Though I find the overall serial lackluster, two features stand out. First, shot on film, Roger Murray-Leach's set is glorious. It looks and feels like a blockbuster movie, which completely changes when shot on video. The back-and-forth of quality inhibits the suspension of disbelief, which makes other weaknesses more apparent. The second feature that stands out is, of course, Tom Baker. He comes off as strange and aloof, and it is fantastic. At times, it's not even clear he's paying attention to the other actors. He stares off into space as though he's an all-wise alien who is bored with their silly human banter. It fits his Doctor perfectly, and with a storyline that is less-than-complex, there is probably good reason for Tom's portrayal.

As you can probably tell, "Planet of Evil" is not my favorite, but it's still good late-night horror. There are some classic *Who* death scenes where actors scream at the air and fall down dead. Underlying the story is the undeveloped critique of energy resources and the need for alternative fuels, which Letts and Dicks would've put center stage. Instead, the mysterious pool that is designed as the centerpiece gets upstaged by Sorenson's anti-matter wolf-man. In fact, the gorgeous outdoor set is eventually ignored for two rooms and a corridor of a spaceship. I typically love Maloney's direction (he directed classics such as "The War Games," "Frontier in Space," "Genesis of the Daleks," and "The Talons of Weng-Chiang"), but "Planet of Evil" seems like a poor remake of "Planet of the Daleks." Ignoring the jungle set in favor of a junky old spaceship might work if the actors were properly directed, but Salamar's and Sorenson's obvious insanity makes the story slow and predictable. Out of the guest actors, Vishinsky (Ewen Solon) is the only character who has a powerful presence.

There are some good aspects of the serial. Tom's alien-esque performance is perfect, and no one can swing a container of anti-matter better. Sarah Jane is also fantastic as usual, and it's nice to see her know what the Doctor needs and be competent enough to find it without any help from the Doctor. There are also some interesting aspects to the story. The space agents have an odd respect for religion, where religious rites are performed but ignored. The Doctor suggests that scientists follow a strict moral code where they are "totally responsible" for the outcomes of their hypotheses—Sorenson eventually kills himself because he's responsible for miscalculating the effect of anti-matter radiation on his cells. There's also the classic duty to respond to a distress signal, which is a great plot device for *Doctor Who*. It's not an episode I would suggest for someone new to *Doctor Who*, but all-in-all, it nicely illustrates several aspects of Classic *Who*.

Pyramids of Mars (1975)
Writer: Stephen Harris
Script Editor: Robert Holmes
Director: Paddy Russell
Producer: Philip Hinchcliffe

Who doesn't love Egyptology and mummies? I don't know why tombs, pharaohs, and mummies are so fascinating, but on October 29, 1983, PBS aired the flawless "Pyramids of Mars." Specific details escape my memory, but I remember being glued to the TV set. Words like 'brilliant' and 'masterpiece' don't get used often in my vocabulary, but this serial deserves both. "Pyramids of Mars" incorporates myth with science fiction, gods with the threat of the universe's destruction, possession, robot mummies, invisible force fields, logic riddles, and so much more. Tom opens the serial alone in the TARDIS console room, fully dressed, and looking down in extreme introspection. He lifts his head, confuses Sarah Jane with Victoria, then talks of walking in eternity. It's one of the greatest scenes in *Doctor Who*, and serves to open one of the best serials. Everyone's performance is top-notch, and the direction includes wonderful elements that incorporate mirror reflections, odd angles, and scene-cuts that leave you guessing about what characters are about to say and do. There's an abundance of outdoor shots that add to the fun and excitement of the show. Every time I watch the scene where the Doctor and Sarah Jane crouch while they walk past the windows, I recall being inspired to do the same when I was a child—everything was an adventure when I was a kid.

The biggest complaint I've ever heard about this serial concerns Sutekh's head/face. Granted, I'm not sure how the "ears" fit in the mask he wears during most of the serial, but I find the head/face rather scary looking—it looks old and weathered, as though it were the face of an evil megalomaniac bent on torturing the universe to death. Speaking of Sutekh's desires, one of the things that makes him a powerful foe is that he seems motivated by nothing more than destruction, which sets him apart from most villains who want adoration, riches, power, etc. His desire for destruction creates a real sense of danger when watching the show, and that the Doctor only determines how to defeat him in the last two minutes of the show is thrilling. It's no wonder Sutekh makes another appearance in the Tenth Doctor's comic book series. So, if you can get past Sutekh's face/head, which only last for ten seconds, "Pyramids of Mars" is a must-see, and if you can't, check out the comic.

What's more, "Pyramids" contains two of my favorite scenes from *Doctor Who*. The first being the logic puzzle the Doctor and Sarah Jane encounter in Sutekh's tomb. The puzzle helped inspire me to study logic, and I now get to ask the question on exams! The second occurs just prior to the logic puzzle, when Scarman and the mummies work on one of their own puzzles. In the background, you see the Doctor and Sarah Jane walk into the scene, then quickly turn around and leave. There's a slapstick sensibility to the scene that makes me laugh every time, and it creates a comfortableness of the characters that makes me smile in delight.

The Android Invasion (1975)
Writer: Terry Nation
Script Editor: Robert Holmes
Director: Barry Letts
Producer: Philip Hinchcliffe

Appearing on PBS November 5, 1983, I remember aspects of "The Android Invasion." I most remember them walking around the town, hanging out in pubs, looking at coins, bug-eyed androids, and running around UNIT headquarters. I've always had a love of androids, so of course, I like the serial. Terry Nation writes a good non-Dalek story, and Barry Letts does a nice job creating some old magic. There are lots of little flubs, like scarves getting caught on limbs and sliding doors not wanting to open. So, if you like to play the drinking game where you have a drink every time a mistake occurs, this is the serial for you. The androids in white, who shoot out of their finger (hmm, wonder where they got that idea) serve to create a nice mystery for the viewer, and Tom and Lis sleuth-it-up like experts. Sarah Jane has a not-so-death-defying drop, and the whole hurt ankle gag makes me cringe. You also get to see a little of UNIT, with Benton and Sullivan, but the Brigadier is oddly missing. Behind the scenes, UNIT was being phased out, and this was their next-to-last appearance until the New Series. Loved how easy it was for the androids' faces to fall off, and Crayford's eye gag (SPOILER: he could see the whole time) never bothered me. Always made me think about how blind we become about ourselves. Finally, you get two Toms in one story, so how could you not like this serial?

The Brain of Morbius (1976)
Writer: "Robin Bland" (Terrance Dicks and Robert Holmes)
Script Editor: Robert Holmes
Director: Christopher Barry
Producer: Philip Hinchcliffe

I'm sure you're tired of me heaping praise on the serials of this season, but I'm not through yet. "The Brain of Morbius" is hands-down, with no hesitation, my favorite *Doctor Who* serial. I can understand why some people find it "bland," but on November 12, 1983, little did I know, but it was one of the most enjoyable 90 minutes of my life. I might have been hopped up on condensed milk and cheese dip, but regardless of the circumstances, "The Brain of Morbius" has always been a favorite. The reasons I love the serial so much are many of the same mentioned above. Tom and Sarah are having fun, running back-and-forth from "witches" (the Sisterhood of Karn) to a mad scientist (Dr. Solon), and of course, the fate of the universe rests on what happens. To dig deeper, the serial's strength lies in its focus on completeness and immortality, seen from different perspectives of the characters. Of course, we know the Doctor is incomplete, wandering the galaxy to fill his life with meaning, but he has a sort of limited immortality. Sarah has found completeness with the Doctor, but her mortality will eventually result in their separation. Condo has no desire for immortality, but is incomplete. The Sisterhood's immortality and completeness is threatened by their inability to sustain their store of the elixir of life. Solon is physically complete, but thrives for the immortality of greatness. Morbius is immortal, but wholly incomplete. Even with Solon's surgeries, Morbius will never be complete, for he's just a bunch of random parts. Surrounding all of these struggles are the dead and mangled bodies of the creatures who crashed on the planet.

Regardless of any shortcomings (e.g., it's only raining in one spot when the Doctor and Sarah Jane stand outside the castle), there is a deepness and creepiness of the serial that make it fun to watch. Tom plays the role as a mouse who is only inches from being gobbled up the entire serial. Tom takes the entire script and set serious, and it pays off to great effect when he engages Morbius in a mental dual. If you remember not liking the serial, give it another shot: turn off the lights, and spend a late night being scared.

The Seeds of Doom (1976)
Writer: Robert Banks Stewart
Script Editor: Robert Holmes
Director: Douglas Camfield
Producer: Philip Hinchcliffe

I have mixed feelings about "Seeds." With space-seeds discovered in Antarctica and man-eating plants, it feels like a Troughton-era story, and the lighting and appearance of UNIT make it feel like a Pertwee-era story. Combined with Hinchcliffe's gothic elements, one would expect this to be ranked as one of the best, but sadly it ends up being the worst serial of the season. "Seeds" starts off strong. The opening two Antarctica episodes are fabulous. They could have easily inspired *Alien* and *The Thing*, and they are just as fun to watch, even though they lack the big budget of a Hollywood film. Tom and Sarah are having fun, alien seeds are possessing humans, and you have a ham-fisted thug killing everyone who gets in the way. I could watch the opening two episodes over and over, and since I don't watch "Seeds" on a regular basis, I often find myself saying, "Why don't I like this serial, these episodes are great!" Sadly, it's while watching the other four episodes that I remember why I'm not a fan.

There are some great moments throughout, and Tom's persistent banter during the serial makes watching it worthwhile. Tony Beckley's character Harrison Chase is fun, especially when he conducts his plant symphony. In fact, his character (and probably the entire story) would fit naturally in a New Series episode and probably be fantastic. The story in itself is not the problem. Like the Antarctica storyline, the garden storyline should've been condensed to two episodes. Instead, you end up with about forty minutes of unnecessary stalling. Don't get me wrong, there are some great moments throughout episodes 3 through 6. Makes me want to go running through the woods, pretending the trees are alive and trying to kill me—like I did when I was a kid. For that fun alone, it's worth watching from time-to-time. So, make sure you give it a shot and see what you think.

As an interesting side note, I didn't see this one when it aired on November 19, 1983, or I did and simply don't remember watching. Nevertheless, this was a special time for *Doctor Who*. Little did I know at the time, but *Doctor Who* was celebrating its 20th Anniversary. Though I missed "Seeds," I did see

"The Five Doctors," which aired Wednesday on PBS, during the evening of November 23, 1983. Can't say much of Tom's participation, except the scenes from "Shada" fit naturally in the first episode. Besides seeing all of the great villains, including the Raston Warrior, "The Five Doctors" introduced me to the concept of regeneration, which unlocked a deep curiosity and fascination about existence. I can't say the extent to which *Doctor Who*'s use of the concept of regeneration affected my life, but it was fairly major. It made me appreciate the vastness and possibilities of reality, which eventually led me to become a philosopher, and for that, I am greatly appreciative.

Season 13 Summation

Season 13 offers some of the best *Doctor Who* available. It illustrates what is possible when creative minds and passionate actors work together. It introduces villains that are mythical in *Doctor Who* lore, many of which continue to appear on television, comics, and novels. The season explores aliens, Egyptology, classic horror, invasions, robots, the environment, anti-matter, fuel shortages, and all sorts of fun things that still tickle the imagination and create a sense of fear. As for my ranking, "Pyramids of Mars" wins top honors, with "Terror of the Zygons" coming in a close second. Both serials do everything you could hope to expect from *Doctor Who*, with villains who are worthy advisories. "The Brain of Morbius" is my personal and sentimental favorite, but even it falls short of the greatness of "Mars" and "Zygons." "The Android Invasion" ranks fourth. With its mystery and odd eye-balled androids, it's an innovative approach to the base-under-siege story that Classic Who does so well. The last two places are split between "Planet of Evil" and "The Seeds of Doom." "Planet" is beautiful, but there are just too many obviously crazy characters who should've been dispensed of earlier. It probably would've worked better being an episode or two shorter. "Seeds" creates a nice atmosphere, especially in the first two episodes and when the Doctor and Sarah are running around outside, but around episode four, the tension turns to tedium, and I'm thinking more of trimming the bushes and raking the leaves than how the Doctor will survive.

Season 13 Ranking

1. Pyramids of Mars
2. Terror of the Zygons
3. The Brain of Morbius
4. The Android Invasion
5. Planet of Evil
6. The Seeds of Doom

Season 14

The Masque of Mandragora (1976)
Writer: Louis Marks
Script Editor: Robert Holmes
Director: Rodney Bennett
Producer: Philip Hinchcliffe

I don't remember much of "The Masque of Mandragora" when it aired on Mississippi PBS, November 26, 1983, but I do recall loving the creepy religious zealots possessed by some weird time vortex energy—the sword fights were pretty cool too. Anytime *Doctor Who* produces a period piece, you can count on the BBC rising to the occasion. "Masque" is no exception. The costumes and locations look great, the catacombs are realistic, and besides the banquet hall at the end, the interiors seem believable. One aspect that makes this period of *Doctor Who* special is that writers and directors allowed for character development. Instead of relying on constant action, you get wonderful scenes of Tom and Lis walking around the TARDIS, talking, joking, and having fun. Their banter creates a sense of enjoyment that makes just about any story enjoyable. When coupled with the fact that "Masque" is a good story, you get a real sense of why *Doctor Who* is still around after almost sixty years.

In terms of specifics, the Helix energy was fun, especially how it fit nicely with the mysticism of the story. Louis Marks develops a nice tension between this mysticism and the emerging Renaissance, which threatens to plunge the human race into a perpetual dark age. It's fun to see the old console room of the TARDIS, and Tom's explanations of the dimensionality of the TARDIS is great for the imagination. There's a real Jonathan and David vibe between Giuliano and Marco that is never explored, and Hieronymous's banter about the moons and stars is a gas. The biggest shortcoming of the serial is that the Doctor appears to execute, or is at least complicit in the execution, of several partygoers. It's hard to tell exactly what happens, but this is what we know. The Doctor is masquerading as the high priest, which means the high priest was out of the picture by the time his acolytes attacked the ball. The person in the lion costume has the Helix energy head, and before this scene the only person with such a head was the high priest; but we've already established that the high priest was out of the picture. So, the Doctor must be in the lion costume, which means he starts the killing, then stands around as his acolytes kill other partygoers. Another explanation is that the high priest survived the previous encounter with the Doctor, dressed up as the lion, and started the killing. This explanation doesn't work because if the high priest were present he would've said something when the Doctor begins to impersonate him. The final option is that some random person, who now has the Helix energy head, dressed up as the lion and started the killing. For this last explanation to work, the Doctor would've had to become the high priest without the others knowing, which seems unlikely, unless the high priest ran to the loo where the Doctor jumped and switched places with him, while the others went up to the party. As you can tell, the last scene really bothers me, and as a result it's hard for me to watch "Masque" without obsessing about the ending. Hopefully, you can still enjoy watching Tom do some fine acting in what's otherwise a great serial.

The Hand of Fear (1976)
Writer: Bob Baker and Dave Martin
Script Editor: Robert Holmes
Director: Lennie Mayne
Producer: Philip Hinchcliffe

Sometimes at conventions I will hear people talk of how they dislike "The Hand of Fear," but I really enjoy it. Tom's performance is serious and heartfelt. Sarah Jane's life is threatened over and over, and each time, Tom convinces viewers that he's genuinely concerned. There's a real sense of friendship and threat of loss, which in the end comes true, because the Doctor must answer an emergency call from the Time Lords. What really makes this episode work is that it never becomes sappy. The threat is real, Sarah Jane is possessed and almost dies several times, and in the end, the Doctor exhibits an all-too-human response to saying goodbye to a friend—he internalizes the loss as though it doesn't affect him. It's a great and powerful moment that becomes a recurring character trait of the Doctor in the New Series. In addition to great acting and writing, there are many nice action scenes, with different camera angles and locations. The alien is fun and strangely seductive, until returned to its "true" form, and the threat of nuclear destruction is always a treat—I grew up in the 80s, when the threat of nuclear destruction was ever-present. Gotta love it when art imitates life.

The Deadly Assassin (1976)
Writer: Robert Holmes
Script Editor: Robert Holmes
Director: David Maloney
Producer: Philip Hinchcliffe

Not a big fan at first, but "The Deadly Assassin" has grown on me over the years. In fact, with all of the murder and political intrigue, the introduction of the Matrix, the reintroduction of the Master, and a glimpse into the mythos of the Time Lords, there's not much to dislike about the serial—except maybe the use of a kiddie train as a means to kill the Doctor. I now consider it one of the best serials of the season. Tom shows he can carry an episode by himself, though he's never again given the opportunity. It's a shame. I've never bought into the idea that you need a companion to make the Doctor relatable and to explain the storyline. Granted, companions offer a nice dimension to the show, but there is something nice about letting the Doctor run the show by himself. Peter Capaldi does a great job as the sole lead in "Heaven Sent." Tom is great in the spotlight, and I wish we could've had a few more episodes with just the Doctor.

The Face of Evil (1977)
Writer: Chris Boucher
Script Editor: Robert Holmes
Director: Pennant Roberts
Producer: Philip Hinchcliffe

"The Face of Evil" is full of great stuff: great set, great concepts, and overall, great cinematography. Tom enters the serial with a strange, but appropriate self-dialogue that not only hints at the Doctor's own mental discombobulation traveling alone, but also foreshadows the schizophrenic state of Xoanon, the artificial intelligence running the planet. Tom's performance is so good that viewers begin the scene thinking it's merely the Doctor breaking the fourth wall, but later realize he's simply lost in his own mind. Just as the difference between talking to oneself and breaking the fourth wall is subtle, the complexity of "The Face of Evil" is subtle and easily missed. A careful viewer will notice the deep philosophical issues of sanity, split-brain theory, artificial intelligence, and other issues relating to the philosophy of mind. Besides some of the special effects, the biggest drawback of the serial is that these philosophical concepts are never fully explored. They are left implied, and though the Doctor mentions a few, they go unaddressed. They are massive issues difficult to conceptualize and discuss, so we shouldn't criticize Chris Boucher or Pennant Roberts for not doing more, but once you start pondering them, it's hard to focus on the story. The story itself is fun, and I like the play on words: Sevateem is the survey team, and the Tesh are the technicians. Leela is a fun addition, even if an odd choice for a companion. She adds a new dimension to the show that hadn't been tried before, and offers a nice challenge to Tom as an actor to explore different aspects of the Doctor's anger, patience, and willingness to guide his new unorthodox companion.

The Robots of Death (1977)
Writer: Chris Boucher
Script Editor: Robert Holmes
Director: Michael E. Briant
Producer: Philip Hinchcliffe

Love, love, love this serial. First saw "The Robots of Death" on December 31, 1983, and it left an indelible mark on my memory. Tom is confident and comfortable, the story is well-written and directed, and the design team's impressive work leaves an unmistakable impression on viewers. There are several nice allusions to classic sci-fi themes, like Asimov's fundamental laws of robots, a nice discussion of the nature of magic vs. the unexplained, and my favorite explanation of why the TARDIS is bigger on the inside—"insides and outsides aren't in the same dimension." There is mystery, murder, commentary on discrimination and slavery, and tension at every turn of the plot. There are pampered rich people getting their comeuppance, possessed robots, and social commentary on slavery. The mining ship and music set a nice tone for the serial, and Tom gets one of his deadly backrubs from the villain—the preferred killing method of Cybermen and Zygons. In fact, this might be the last attempt to kill the Fourth Doctor with a backrub. I could go on-and-on about how much I love the episode, but I'll spare you the details. If you've not seen it, do it now!

The Talons of Weng-Chiang (1977)
Writer: Robert Holmes
Script Editor: Robert Holmes
Director: David Maloney
Producer: Philip Hinchcliffe

For some, this is their favorite serial of *Doctor Who*. It premiered in 1977, the year I was born, though I doubt my parents were even aware of *Doctor Who*'s existence. A few years later during the winter of 1984, I vaguely remember watching "Talons." In fact, this might have been the last serial I saw on PBS until the 1990s, though it's possible I saw bits of "The Sun Makers," "Underworld," and "The Leisure Hive" later in 1984—I have vague memories that might be real or just imagined. The serial itself has a great atmosphere that recalls foggy London streets, hints of Scotland Yard, and of course,

Sherlock Holmes. It's no wonder Victorian England is often where writers place the Fourth Doctor—it's the setting for multiple comics, audios, and novels. "Talons" involves a fun mystery with magic, the Doctor's rekindled Venusian Aikido, and everyone's favorite, a giant rat. For the most part, "Talons" is a great story, but it has its problems. Robert Holmes wrote the script and most of it is spot-on, but parts of it feel rushed and contrived. According to Richard Molesworth's biography of Robert Holmes, Holmes didn't like six-part stories, and struggled to finish the script on time. Some scenes were quickly added at the last minute.

The other problem is the serial's use of stereotypes and actors in "yellowface" in order to simulate Asian characters. As a younger viewer, I paid no attention to this feature of the serial. In fact, I thought Li H'sen Chang's strange appearance was because he was an alien. His face is similar to Mr Sin's puppet face, so I thought maybe it was part of their disguises on Earth. As an older viewer, the use of yellowface just seems odd and lazy, but it was a common practice for the time; and in some cases, it is still common. Is it racist? That's a topic for a different venue. Is it offensive? Yes, because anytime you use a character to paint a caricature of another race or ethnic group, you fail to provide an accurate representation. John Bennett plays Li H'sen Chang with respect, and even if the majority of viewers at the time didn't care; for contemporary viewers and those from the caricaturized group, there's an instant disconnect and feeling of being mocked when non-native actors portray your group.

The third and final problem is Leela. Her character devolves from what we saw in previous serials. To be honest, most of the characters in the serial are portrayed in a negative light. Henry Jago is a money-grubbing fool, George Litefoot is a pompous dolt, and the list goes on. Holmes wanted to spotlight Tom, and besides the Doctor, the main villains are the only competent characters, and they all get defeated. So, for a serial I used to love dearly, I feel as though its standing has dropped over the years. Yet, Tom's performance is admirable and worth the watch.

Season 14 Summation

Season 14 is an interesting season. There really isn't a weak episode, several of the serials feature the same writer and director, and there are at least two "classic" serials, yet I rarely hear fans rank Season 14 as one of their favorites. It might simply be overshadowed by the previous two seasons, but as I recently re-watched Season 14, I found myself quite impressed with the complexity of concepts in the stories, and besides some of the cringeworthy moments here and there, the rest of the season is spotless. There are definitely some sad moments, as we're forced to say goodbye to Sarah Jane Smith, but even that is handled quite well. Of course, as I think back to watching some of these episodes for the first time, I remember being confused about the Doctor being alone, Leela's role in the show, and why the Doctor kept her on the TARDIS; but as a kid, ultimately, none of these things mattered. Looking at these serials with full knowledge of Leela's story-arc, she brings a certain air of hopefulness to the show, and though she is under-/mis-used in future serials, Leela fits perfectly in this season. So, if you remember not liking the season, give it another shot. Yes, it's the end of the Holmes/Hinchcliffe era, but they went out in style with a genuinely strong season.

"The Robots of Death" is an easy choice for best serial. I generally have a fetish for robots, and I find these to be a master-example of how robots should look. Add in a good story and some strange characters, and this is *Doctor Who* at its best. "The Deadly Assassin" comes in second, with "The Talons of Weng-Chiang" a close third. "Talons" offers a nice period piece, with the Doctor showing off his Sherlock skills and Leela playing a less-than-flattering fish-out-of-water. "The Deadly Assassin" gives viewers a nice political drama, with a dash of psychological thriller. Both are fun to watch on a dark rainy night with the lights turned low. With its direction, old-school action scenes, and plot, "The Hand of Fear" gains my number four spot. "Masque" comes in at number five, though if you asked me a few years back, I probably would have ranked it higher. I really struggle with the ending, where the Doctor seems to kill/let be killed several innocent people. "The Face of Evil" comes in sixth, mainly due to its direction. They tackle some serious conceptual issues dealing with artificial intelligence, psychopathy, fundamentalism, and among many more, the philosophy of mind. Even the best director would struggle with this script, yet Pennant Roberts does a decent job. Overall, a great season of Tom and *Doctor Who*, and the last of an important era in Who history.

Season 14 Ranking

1. The Robots of Death
2. The Deadly Assassin
3. The Talons of Weng-Chiang
4. The Hand of Fear
5. The Masque of Mandragora
6. The Face of Evil

Season 15

Horror of Fang Rock (1977)
Writer: Terrance Dicks
Script Editor: Robert Holmes
Director: Paddy Russell
Producer: Graham Williams

Terrance Dicks returns with a spooky lighthouse-under-siege story. Leela does some killing, wears appropriate clothes, and has her eye color changed—a production decision that allowed Louise Jameson to use her natural eye color instead of brown contacts. Tom battles a Rutan, the ancient foe of the Sontarans, explains things to shipwrecked elites, who are often the Rutan in disguise, and navigates claustrophobic staircases. There's nothing especially deep about the story, but it is a fun monster story, similar to the gothic style of the Hinchcliffe era. It's also a great example of everyone dying in a serial, which becomes especially relevant in the New Series. Tom's portrayal is mysterious and sympathetic, working hard to reason with the Rutan, though at the same time being belligerent—"oyster face." As a side note, Terrance Dicks passed away as I prepared this review, so I feel it appropriate to say: Thank you, Terrance, for all you did (and he did a bunch) to make *Doctor Who* special.

The Invisible Enemy (1977)
Writer: Bob Baker and Dave Martin
Script Editor: Robert Holmes
Director: Derrick Goodwin
Producer: Graham Williams

With "Horror of Fang Rock" seeming like a continuation of the Hinchcliffe era, "The Invisible Enemy" feels like something new. There's a new color palette for the spaceship, and there's a definite sci-fi feel to Graham Williams's production. Leela exhibits an ability to sense danger, which works well with the Doctor's reliance on factual methods. The serial introduces some interesting concepts relating to cloning, viruses, artificial intelligence, and traveling inside one's own body—*Fantastic Voyage*-esque. The serial is strong, and it's fun to watch Tom play a double agent, until he becomes self-comatose, in order to prevent the spread of The Nucleus. The Nucleus is an interesting idea that works well until it's actually introduced on screen. The blob in the Doctor's brain works, but when it escapes and grows into a fully formed being, I can't help but become hungry for shrimp! Not sure of the design decisions that went into making The Nucleus, but they couldn't have been happy about its outcome. Even if we look past its shrimpiness, the fact it is led around by its arms makes it hard to suspend disbelief and enjoy its presence. Speaking of struggling to suspend disbelief, the gun fighting is unbearable. They would've better better off deleting the little laser-bursts and just having the noises. Even with its shortcomings, "The Invisible Enemy" is a fun serial with some nice acting by Tom, some neat glimpses of what's to come in the following serials, and of course, the introduction of K-9, who will become a fan-favorite and a close companion of the Doctor.

Image of the Fendahl (1977)
Writer: Chris Boucher
Script Editor: Robert Holmes
Director: George Spenton-Foster
Producer: Graham Williams

The "Image of the Fendahl" has conniving scientists drunk with the possibility of glory, pentagrams, séances, aliens, and of course, a threat to human civilization. In other words, it has the perfect ingredients for a classic *Doctor Who* serial, and "Image" doesn't disappoint. There are some great moments when Tom's legs won't work, and he has to convince them to start running. Leela has a new outfit that somehow keeps everything covered (and somehow made it past Standards and Practices). What makes this serial stand out is the cast and George Spenton-Foster's attention to detail on the set. The supporting cast is strong and convincing, with believable characters that pique the interest of viewers. Even the evil scientist who's part of the coven, Max Stael, generates sympathy before the Doctor helps him commit suicide, instead of being taken over by the Fendahl. The supporting cast simply shines. As for detail, there is a creepy live owl hiding on one set and the homes, scientific labs, and séance sets are all convincing. The Fendahline are basically The Nucleus from "The Invisible Enemy," but their worm-like appearance works in this serial. The fan-blowing tentacles are a nice touch too. One last detail that I enjoyed was that Thea Ransome (the scientists possessed by the Fendahl) actually visits the Doctor for help, prior to becoming a full-blown murdering alien, but because the Doctor had previously escaped, he was unable to help prevent the resulting disaster. This adds a touch of tragedy to the serial of which the other characters are unaware. Tom provides a nice performance, especially of being oblivious to Leela's new, in-your-face outfit, and when you put it all together, this is a great serial.

The Sun Makers (1977)
Writer: Robert Holmes
Script Editor: Anthony Read
Director: Pennant Roberts
Producer: Graham Williams

Besides learning that the Doctor cheats in chess, "The Sun Makers" leaves no doubt about Bob Holmes's feelings towards the "tax man." With biting social commentary, "The Sun Makers" illustrates science fiction's ability to allegorize the world we inhabit. Barry Letts and Terrance Dicks were masters of this approach, and Holmes shows he is too. What makes the story especially interesting is that both the rebels and the bureaucrats are portrayed as buffoons. Thankfully, Tom grounds the episode with an air of nonchalance, and even though he's constantly getting caught (from the obvious "ATM" trap to him accidently waking up the guard), he's always in control.

Tom's approach to the serial allows viewers to pay attention to other aspects, such as the humor and farce of the whole thing. The serial does tackle some troubling political issues, demonstrating how economic power is more efficient than war. The government makes people dependent on taxes, then taxes them until they cease to be profitable. Once no longer profitable, they're allowed to die, but this death only serves to make others dependent on taxes. It's no wonder workers are willing to commit suicide. On the other hand, taxes and work often rob individuals of the free time to seek other means of self-development, such as education. So, you end up with a set of rebels sitting around being ignorant and lazy. The Doctor leaves them with high hopes of returning to Earth, but I'm afraid this lot might not even be able to feed themselves. They will probably spend most of their time throwing people they don't like over the sides of buildings, which is always a shocking scene to watch in the serial. I guess it's this mixture that makes me like the serial so much.

Underworld (1978)
Writer: Bob Baker and Dave Martin
Script Editor: Anthony Read
Director: Norman Stewart
Producer: Graham Williams

The quest is the quest! You heard me, and besides some not-so-special effects, "Underworld" is an otherwise fantastic, Jason and the Argonauts-inspired serial. Leela is back in her revealing costume and flying the TARDIS, while the Doctor busies himself by painting who-knows-what, until they reach the edge of the cosmos and join a millennia-old crew on a quest to rescue their lost race-bank from the *P7E*. What you get is a fantastic sci-fi space drama, with a nice supporting cast (especially on the spaceship) that make the serial believable, in spite of the special effects. Even Tom gets into things, spouting the mantra, "the quest is the quest."

Other remarkable aspects of the serial include the effective use of K-9 throughout much of the story. The Seers' costumes are nicely done, presenting a creepy spider-eye effect, and when they reveal their domed heads, they rank as one of my favorite costumes. Next, if you take into account the themes of "The Sunmakers," "Underworld" offers a striking critique of mining corporations. Finally, the serial gives viewers a glimpse into Time Lord mythology by discussing the God-like power they control and why they now have a strict policy of non-intervention. So, even with its Styrofoam rocks, digital cave scenes, and the Doctor saying "shut up" to his friends (it always makes me cringe), "Underworld" offers up a pleasant sci-fi adaptation of an already great mythological story. They should have done one of *Medea* next, but *Medea* doesn't have such a happy ending; so, it's probably best they didn't.

The Invasion of Time (1978)
Writer: David Agnew (David Fisher, Douglas Adams, and Graham Williams)
Script Editor: Anthony Read
Director: Gerald Blake
Producer: Graham Williams

Tom brings Season 15 to an exciting end with "The Invasion of Time." "Invasion" takes viewers back to Gallifrey where the Doctor seeks to claim his title of Lord President. Tom plays the Doctor as unstable and erratic, which fits the storyline perfectly. Speaking of perfect, John Arnatt's portrayal of Borusa is out of this world. I'm instantly sympathetic towards the character, and feel truly betrayed in "The Five Doctors," when he becomes the villain. Another nice aspect of the serial is that Leela is given a secondary story where she meets the "savage" tribes of Gallifrey. She also gets to take down some Sontarans. Her storyline works well with the Doctor's erratic behavior, which viewers know is some sort of ruse; but it's fun to watch and try and figure out what angle he's playing. Of course, the laugh-out-loud moment is when Tom breaks the fourth wall and says, "Even the sonic screwdriver won't get me out of this one."

In general, I always enjoy learning Time Lord mythology, so it's exciting to see them return to Gallifrey in Classic *Doctor Who*. The serial also creates a little TARDIS mythology by giving viewers a glimpse of its infiniteness. The best part of the serial is when episode four ends. You think it's over, and the Doctor's about to make his normal exit, then the Sontarans arrive and reveal their strategy for invasion. It was fabulous the first time I saw it in the late 90s, and even after seeing it multiple times, this complete shift in the story is still fun. Of course, when all is said and done, the serial ends with Leela staying on Gallifrey. She's in love and stays behind with K-9. It's fun to think about what sort of impact she made on Gallifrey. I always imagine it's her and Andred who help the Tenth Doctor in "The End of Time" (2009). With Leela and K-9 gone, it appears to be a sad ending, until Tom reveals K-9 Mark II, looks at the camera and gives viewers a nice big smile. His adventures are far from over, and it's the perfect way to end the serial and season.

Season 15 Summation

Season 15 is another strong season of *Doctor Who*. Even its weakest serial is fun and engaging. Williams's new approach shines throughout, but there are constant hints of "old-school" *Doctor Who*. One can't help but think of 1960's *Doctor Who* when seeing The Nucleus, which might have worked better in black and white. "The Sun Makers" and "Image of the Fendahl" scream Pertwee, Letts, and Dicks. Simply stated, 15 is a good season with strong acting by Tom Baker and the final development of Leela, there's little to nothing to dislike.

"The Sun Makers" is ranked number one. The serial is fun, different, and full of real-life issues, like taxes, corporate bureaucracy, and suicide. Holmes delivers a great script that is well-acted and produced. "The Image of Fendhal" comes in at number two with its ancient aliens and mysticism. It's spooky, keeps the story going with twists and turns, and makes for classic screenings of late-night *Doctor Who*. I know some will disagree, but "The Invasion of Time" wins third place. I love how drastically it changes storylines from one story to the next. The entrance of the Sontarans is like the Spanish Inquisition—No one expects the Spanish Inquisition! The Doctor is all over the place, and it makes for a great serial. "The Invisible Enemy" ranks fourth, with "Underworld" coming in at a close fifth. "The Invisible Enemy" is fun and refreshing, toys with some interesting ideas, and introduces K-9, while "Underworld" recreates Greek mythology; both of which work nicely. Finally, "Horror of Fang Rock" ranks sixth, with its fun under-siege story that has implications for the rest of the Whoniverse. Overall, Season 15 of *Doctor Who* is quite strong, with nice performances by Tom and Louise.

Season 15 Ranking

1. The Sun Makers
2. Image of the Fendahl
3. The Invasion of Time
4. The Invisible Enemy
5. Underworld
6. Horror of Fang Rock

Season 16

The Ribos Operation (1978)
Writer: Robert Holmes
Script Editor: Anthony Read
Director: George Spenton-Foster
Producer: Graham Williams

Besides serving as an introduction to the Key to Time series, "The Ribos Operation" is a self-contained story that benefits from superb character acting. As you might expect, Tom is great. He plays the highs and lows of being forced into an errand by the "White" Guardian and taking on a new companion, who happens to be way smarter and just as charming. Instead of being mean, as he was with Harry Sullivan, Tom plays the part as a disappointed child, using sarcasm and wit to deflect Romana's intrusion into his life. What results is thoroughly enjoyable banter. Romana explains the Doctor's actions with clinical psychobabble, the Doctor childishly dismisses the accusation, then continues to confirm her diagnosis with his actions. Mary Tamm is fantastic, and she sets a wonderful tone for the entire season. Makes me wish she stayed around for a few more!

Tamm is not the only great addition to "Ribos." Garron and Unstoffe are the stars of the serial, and they make the sub-stories engaging and fun. Wish they could've made a few more appearances during Tom's run on the show. Of course, what makes the serial work is that Robert Holmes and George Spenton-Foster create a genuine sense of being conned. Bad guys rip-off bad guys, the Doctor and Romana switch sides multiple times, and Tom even masquerades as the one of the Graff's guards. Sleight of hand tricks are abundant throughout, the two most prominent examples being when the Doctor and Graff double-switch the rare mineral (the Key to Time segment) and the Doctor places the bomb on Graff. I can imagine some viewers criticizing the Doctor for letting the Graff blow himself up, without showing any concern, but the real criticism is that he seems to fall for The White Guardian's story about the Key to Time. He should've known something was wrong, when this semi-all-powerful being is incapable of getting the pieces himself. Maybe the Doctor knew the whole time. I'd like to think so, especially since Tom portrays the Doctor as completely unconcerned with the segments to the Key to Time. Regardless, "Ribos" is a great start to another fun-filled season.

The Pirate Planet (1978)
Writer: Douglas Adams
Script Editor: Anthony Read
Director: Pennant Roberts
Producer: Graham Williams

Douglas Adams makes his writing debut on *Doctor Who* with "The Pirate Planet," and he presents fans with a fun and intriguing story. The serial finds the Doctor and Romana looking for the second segment of the Key to Time on a planet ruled by a mad space pirate. Precious stones are everywhere ignored, a strange cult converts young adults to their yellow-clad mental crusade, and K-9 battles a robotic parrot. Planets are condensed into trophies held in stasis fields, similar to Series Eleven's finale in the New Series, the true villain is obscured as a nurse, and everyone goes home happy—except the billions killed in the process of destroying various planets. I've heard some complain that the acting is over-the-top, but I find it quirky and fun. For those familiar with Adams's approach to humor and sci-fi, the serial is quite restrained. I've also heard some complain about the robotic parrot, but for what was available at the time, the parrot creates a fun diversion that lets K-9 be the hero. Tom is playful and relaxed, which creates a relaxed atmosphere where viewers are able to relax and enjoy watching their favorite Time Lord save Earth once again.

The Stones of Blood (1978)
Writer: David Fisher
Script Editor: Anthony Read
Director: Darrol Blake
Producer: Graham Williams

Stonehenge was a great fascination of mine growing up, so I instantly took a liking to "The Stones of Blood" and its "Nine Travelers." With fantastic acting, wonderful story, and a creepiness highlighted by the senseless murder of two campers, "Stones" is one of the Tom Baker era's best serials. David Fisher brings together multiple elements, including mythology, archeology, escaped criminals, bloodthirsty rocks, and among others, courtroom drama to create an atmosphere where the actors shine. Everyone's character is believable, and there's a real sense of tension when it appears that the Doctor will lose his case. The villain Cessair is turned into a stone, and the Doctor and Romana recover the Key to Time segment. "Stones" is perfect late-night *Doctor Who* horror, with just a pinch of sci-fi to delight fans.

The Androids of Tara (1978)
Writer: David Fisher
Script Editor: Anthony Read
Director: Michael Hayes
Producer: Graham Williams

"The Androids of Tara" is more romp than anything else. The Doctor is more interested in playing chess and going fishing than searching for the Key to Time. In fact, the Key to Time seems like a last-minute addition. Romana finds the segment within the first few minutes, it plays no role in the story, and then it reappears at the end. What makes the serial enjoyable is that it's mostly four episodes of Tom having fun. Tom is so relaxed in his portrayal of the Doctor that his performance has the feeling of being unscripted. The banter between Romana and the Doctor continues to be exceptional, and even K-9 gets in on the fun—until he's abandoned on a boat! The android duplications are fun, and though having a princess that looks exactly like Romana stretches the limits of believability, they all work together fairly well. The serial would've benefited by being one episode shorter, but it's still worth the watch.

The Power of Kroll (1978-1979)
Writer: Robert Holmes
Script Editor: Anthony Read
Director: Norman Stewart
Producer: Graham Williams

Kroll, Kroll, Kroll, Kroll… "The Power of Kroll" is one of my favorites. From the model oilrig, which is underwhelming until Kroll pops out of the water to gobble it up, to the natives in green paint, the serial is just fun. It benefits from a great locale, with story elements that allow the Doctor to fashion a flute out of a reed, Romana to make quirky remarks and observations, and for the story to unfold at a proper pace. Written by Bob Holmes, "Kroll" critiques colonialism, religion, and humanity in general. As is common with a Holmes story, the Doctor seems miles beyond everyone else in intelligence and understanding. For instance, while Romana and Rohm-Dutt are worrying about being killed, the Doctor is engaged in delightful banter about architecture, while calculating the strength of the glass and the pitch of voice required for it to break. Tom is passionate and spouts off his technobabble lines like an expert, while critiquing both progress as a "flexible word" and the manufactured "miracles" of the religious "natives." There's some great dialogue that's easily missed, if you don't pay attention, such as

Romana's talk of "displacement anxiety" after her nose stops itching, the Doctor trying to get things "straightened out," and several discussions about the rituals of death—the first ritual being when "they just throw you down the pit and drop rocks on you." I can see where some would think the serial slow, but I find the pacing quite pleasant. I also don't care that the "Swampies" are obviously painted. I never thought they were green aliens. It makes more sense that they simply painted themselves with dyes from their natural environment. Heck, I'm even okay with the CSO overlay. Yeah, when Kroll fills the skyline, it's obviously fake; but I find it a good fake. The only issue I have is when the Doctor goes to test his hunch about Kroll being the segment. All he had to do was touch any part of Kroll and Kroll would've changed. There was no need for him to wrestle with the tentacles. Maybe it was Holmes's way of paying homage to Bela Lugosi's notorious tentacle scene in Ed Wood's *Bride of the Monster*. Regardless, if you've never seen it and only hear bad things about it, give it another shot.

The Armageddon Factor (1979)
Writer: Bob Baker and Dave Martin
Script Editor: Anthony Read
Director: Michael Hayes
Producer: Graham Williams

The "New" *Who* of the late 70's is in full effect by "The Armageddon Factor." With a certain level of humor and escapism, the Key to Time arc comes to an exciting climax with this serial. Beginning with the escapism of an over-dramatic melodrama of two star-crossed lovers, "The Armageddon Factor" illustrates the lunacy of megalomania and war in general. Tom provides a lively performance, especially when he completes the Key to Time and becomes "evil." K-9, Romana, and the soon to be Romana II get in on the action and create a fantastic tale of science fiction. Besides the obvious craziness of The Marshall, who would've been relieved of duty in normal circumstances, the serial is believable and at times intense. Something else that's really cool, we learn the Doctor's name—at least one of his earlier names—when the Doctor's old schoolmate, Drax, calls him Theta Sigma, or Thete for short—Class of 92! Is this his birth name? Who knows, but it's a fun throwaway line that is often ignored or unknown by fans.

In regard to this being the last serial in the Key to Time series, in interviews, Tom has discussed how he was skeptical of the effectiveness of a season-long story arc, but I for one like how the stories interconnect. Each serial is both varied and introduces a wide range of villains and situations. Tom and Mary Tamm are great throughout, and the Key to Time arc would fit perfectly within the New Series. Another reason for recognizing the groundbreaking work of *Doctor Who*.

Season 16 Summation

The serialization of Season 16 works for me, and it's probably the best later season of Tom's run as the Doctor. Not to say the next two seasons aren't enjoyable, in fact some of the best serials of Tom's tenure occur in Seasons 17 and 18, but they don't work as well as previous seasons. Even though I might be persuaded to say Season 17 is better, I tend to favor Season 16 because of its interconnectedness and overall fun-factor. Romana and K-9 shine throughout, and Williams's sci-fi vision of *Doctor Who* creates a series-defining approach. Tom is energetic and continues his life-changing performance as the greatest of all Time Lords. Whether fighting a swamp beast like the Kroll, or planet-shrinking pirates (whose tactics resemble those featured in "The Battle of Ranskoor Av Kolos"), Season 16 holds up to the best of *Doctor Who*.

"The Pirate Planet," with its clever notion of shrinking planets, oppression, and of course a robot parrot, ranks as my number one. Douglas Adams provides a nice story that works on multiple levels. Taking into account the performance of the actors, it's simply a great example of sci-fi television. "The Stones of Blood" comes in second. It's a fun historically-based story that speculates about the nature of ancient Stonehenge-like structures, a personal favorite historical curiosity. The serial includes great actors, a fun story, and a challenging courtroom drama. The Doctor narrowly escapes, and the villain is strangely seductive, which seems to affect the Doctor in no way.

With its tribal religion and modern-day lessons about mining, "The Power of Kroll" ranks third. It's just a fun story with lots of great situations that threaten to destroy the Doctor at every turn. "The Ribos Operation" comes in at four, with "The Armageddon Factor" at five. "Ribos" starts the Key to Time arc with a jewel heist, human greed, and great acting. "The Armageddon Factor" ends the arc with nuclear war and the summation of a yearlong story. There's little to complain about in either episode. So, why not sit back and enjoy both. "The Androids of Tara," with its romp through "medieval Europe," ranks sixth. With several twists and turns, it's hard not to enjoy "Tara." Tom finds a way to entertain and still find the key to time, which is no different than any other *Doctor Who* story. So, what's not to enjoy?

Season 16 Ranking

1. The Pirate Planet
2. The Stones of Blood
3. The Power of Kroll
4. The Ribos Operation
5. The Armageddon Factor
6. The Androids of Tara

Season 17

Destiny of the Daleks (1979)
Writer: Terry Nation
Script Editor: Douglas Adams
Director: Ken Grieve
Producer: Graham Williams

"Destiny of the Daleks" is a great start to Season 17, Tom's penultimate season. Tom is lively and charming, and the new companion, Romana II, promises to be just as engaging, witty, confident, and competent as Romana I. Douglas Adams has taken over as script editor, so there's greater emphasis on humor and catchy storylines, both of which complement Graham Williams sci-fi aesthetic. Examples such as when Tom reads and critiques a history of the universe while patiently lying underneath a concrete column, or when the Doctor responds to Romana's esoteric knowledge of spaceships with, "Without reference to my *Jane's Spacecrafts of the Universe*, I wouldn't dispute that," illustrate Adams's impact on the show.

Of course, "Destiny" features the Daleks, which viewers hadn't seen in five years, but it also reintroduces Davros as the creator of the Daleks, who will become a recurring, impossible-to-kill villain. Davros's reappearance introduces two more aspects that will become part of the *Doctor Who* mythology: 1) there's a rift in the Daleks between those loyal to Davros and those loyal to the Supreme Dalek; and 2) the Daleks have a natural enemy in the Movellans, who are just as good at strategic warfare. A credit to the serial is that both Davros and the Movellans will eventually make their way into the New Series. Finally, Ken Grieve's direction offers viewers nice actions shots, effective lighting, and good costuming. I've always been amazed by the androgynous nature of the Movellans. They effectively obscure gender, creating a sleek sexiness that matchers their android nature and serves as a nice counterpoint to the clunky, unattractive Daleks.

With the start of a new season, "Destiny" suggests a new direction for *Doctor Who*, one that is further supported by the following two serials ("City of Death" and "The Creature from the Pit"). Unfortunately, this new direction is the exception, not the rule. For whatever the reason, and there are several theories, the season is inconsistent. As a result, instead of being a glimpse into the future direction of the show, "Destiny" becomes an homage to the potential greatness of *Doctor Who* and marks the beginning of the end of Tom's portrayal of the Doctor.

City of Death (1979)
Writer: "David Agnew" (David Fisher, Douglas Adams, and Graham Williams)
Script Editor: Douglas Adams
Director: Michael Hayes
Producer: Graham Williams

There's not much to say about "City of Death," except that it is one of the best serials of *Doctor Who*. It is expertly written, as it should be, since David Fisher, Douglas Adams, and Graham Williams all played a role in its creation. The direction is fun, the location shots create a real sense of adventure, and the acting is phenomenal—including a guest appearance by none other than the great John Cleese. Tom and Lalla exude a bond that adds a new dimension to the show, one that will become an ongoing theme in 1980s television shows like *Moonlighting*, *Remington Steele*, and *Cheers*. The producers could've really played up the love story angle for several seasons, but for some reason, it never fully materializes. I guess they thought it too radical.

Besides a debonair alien disguised as a human, an art heist, and tons of Adams-style humor, the sci-fi plot is fairly ingenious. The characters all seem concerned with the Mona Lisa, while in fact, the real concern is that human evolution might be prevented. Instead, Scaroth's attempt to escape sparks human evolution and creates an endless cycle where he's destined to relive the story of the serial for all eternity—gotta love time-loops! With nothing negative to say, "City of Death" is a great serial for all audiences.

The Creature from the Pit (1979)
Writer: David Fisher
Script Editor: Douglas Adams
Director: Christopher Barry
Producer: Graham Williams

"The Creature from the Pit" has all the makings of a great serial. There's fun banter between the Doctor, Romana, and K-9. There's a nice set, and the Wolfweeds are a neat concept. The fact the creature is an alien ambassador and not just a mindless animal creates a nice tension throughout the serial, as viewers try to figure out what the Lady Adrasta is concealing. Geoffrey Bayldon's character Organon is a fabulous element, and Tom exhibits a wide range of emotions, as the Doctor is sometimes curious and playful, and at other times amazed and confused. So, where does it go wrong? David Fisher's script has several strong components, especially in terms of the main story's plot, twists, and turns. Where it goes afoul is the introduction and use of the bandits. They are ridiculous and serve no purpose in the story. Sure, they steal the fragment that powers the alien's ship, but anyone could've caused the fragment to go missing—Karela, the Huntsman, or a random guard. It's just a shame to have an otherwise great script and serial suffer from something so unnecessary, but at least we find out that the Doctor's lucky number is 74,384,338.

Nightmare of Eden (1979)
Writer: Bob Baker
Script Editor: Douglas Adams
Director: Alan Bromly
Producer: Graham Williams

Come on! You can see human faces in the costumes of the Mandrels on the cover of the DVD! This is either the creative consultants on vraxion, or the greatest ever nod to *Doctor Who*'s fantastic "cheapness." Regardless, "Nightmare of Eden" is the story of two ships getting stuck during a hyperspace materialization, which then creates a set of cascading problems for the drug smugglers on board. Enter the Doctor, who masquerades with Romana and K-9 as secret agents. Tom is superb, and the serial offers a nice examination of drugs, corruption, and humanity's love of bureaucracy. There's also room for a discussion about the ethics of zoos, some really nice writing about the possibility of two ships becoming entangled on a quantum level, and well-done special effects for *Doctor Who*. Of course, the exaggerated German accent is a dead giveaway for the villain, but even this "gaffe" provides an entertaining aspect to an overall fun serial.

The Horns of Nimon (1979-1980)
Writer: Anthony Read
Script Editor: Douglas Adams
Director: Kenny McBain
Producer: Graham Williams

I've heard many fans bash "The Horns of Nimon," mainly due to the set design and acting. I get it, there's a lot not to be desired about the serial. In fact, there's an absence of "magic" in the serial—whatever "magic" means. The story doesn't create an atmosphere where viewers are absorbed in the episodes. With the privilege of hindsight, maybe this was a sign that Tom, Graham Williams, and the show itself was in need of a fresh approach; or maybe it's due to other episodes being so strong; but there's something a little off about the serial. Nevertheless, I like the story, Graham Crowden's over-the-top performance as Soldeed is fun, and I like the Nimon costume. It's a little clunky, but as seen in the Matt Smith-era episode "The God Complex," the costume and character can work quite effectively. With its stark colors and reused corridors, the serial might have worked better in black and white. Who knows? It's still a decent story, just under-inspired. Tom provides some great scenes, including some humorous appearing/disappearing gags in the transporter "egg," and you get to see the Nimon lumber around. For those reasons alone, it's worth a watch.

Shada (Never Broadcast)
Writer: Douglas Adams
Script Editor: Douglas Adams
Director: Pennant Roberts
Producer: Graham Williams

Besides being incomplete and there existing fifteen different versions (VHS, DVDs, books, animated, enhanced, etc.), "Shada" is still a great serial. With hindsight, this should've been Tom's last outing. The energy, excitement, and magic witnessed from Tom, Lalla, and the rest of the crew never appears again after "Shada." Sadly, "Shada" would never be completed, and so, never aired. Of course, there have been multiple attempts to complete the unfinished work, the most recent featuring reanimated scenes and the special appearance of Tom at the end. All of these are special in their own way, and contribute to the mystique of the serial; they fall short of what could've been one of Tom's most memorable serials, especially if Tom had ended his journey on such a high note.

Season 17 Summation

Fantastic but inconsistent. From all accounts, Douglas Adams tended to spread himself thin, so it's no wonder some episodes are better than others. Of course, Adams can't be blamed for all of the season's shortcomings. In fact, it's not clear the "shortcomings" are actual shortcomings. Each story has its strengths and virtues, but there's something off about the season as a whole. The season is more cohesive than Season 18, but upon reflection, this would've been the perfect time for Tom to end his run, assuming they finished filming "Shada."

"City of Death" ranks as number one, illustrating the best of *Doctor Who*. Inventive and fun, there's nothing that compares to "City." "Nightmare of Eden" ranks second, mainly because of its social message. It provides a nice critique of zoos, drugs, and the "war on drugs," and gives the cast several opportunities to shine. "Destiny of the Daleks" ranks a close third, and could easily replace "Eden" as number two. There's humor, Daleks, and Davros, with a good story and fun acting. "The Creature from the Pit" ranks fourth, and would rank higher if not for the bandits—they really undermine the story. "The Horns of Nimon" ranks fifth. It falls flat, especially when compared with the other stories. Finally, "Shada" comes in sixth place, only because it is unfinished. I was tempted to rank it number two, but with elements missing, it seemed unfair. Of course, the animated version completes the story and adds a new appearance from Tom Baker, so I'm sure I could be convinced to give it a higher rank, especially over a pint.

Season 17 Ranking

1. City of Death
2. Nightmare of Eden
3. Destiny of the Daleks
4. The Creature from the Pit
5. The Horns of Nimon
6. Shada (though as high as 2, if completed)

Season 18

The Leisure Hive (1980)
Writer: David Fisher
Script Editor: Christopher H. Bidmead
Director: Lovett Bickford
Producer: John Nathan-Turner

I have a vague feeling I saw "The Leisure Hive" when I was a child (the only possible date is June 23, 1984), which is probably because John Nathan-Turner's (JNT) inaugural episode as producer is a fun foray towards a new direction for *Doctor Who*. JNT wanted to move the show into the 80s, and he does a good job with the serial. The new opening title sequence is flashy and good, the Doctor's new outfit is a nice tweak of his old one, and there's a new feel to the show. Lighting and camera filters create a new atmosphere in which to enjoy everyone's favorite Time Lord. "The Leisure Hive" itself benefits from a good story, great makeup, and set design. The costumes are great, and the Leisure Hive is believable. The Foamasi costumes work fairly well, and the aged Doctor's makeup is fantastically realistic. Tom's performance is strong, and there's a nice strangeness to the serial that offers viewers hope in the future of *Doctor Who*.

Meglos (1980)
Writer: John Flanagan and Andrew McCulloch
Script Editor: Christopher H. Bidmead
Director: Terrance Dudley
Producer: John Nathan-Turner

"Meglos" is memorable for several reasons, including a cactus Doctor and more importantly Jacqueline Hill's (a.k.a. the First Doctor's companion, Barbara Wright) return to the show. In fact, the guest stars steal the show. Hill does a nice job as the stern religious zealot, Lexa, who compliments Edward Underdown's patient sage-like character, Zastor. On the villain side of things, Tom gets to be the baddie Meglos, and Christopher Owen has presence as the abducted Earthling. Of course, Bill Fraser and Frederick Treves offer inspired performances of their respective characters, General Grugger and Lieutenant Brotadac. Besides the fact Meglos-as-a-cactus, with his obvious mobility issues being a cactus, needs the help from outsiders, the Gaztak pirates are unnecessary. Nevertheless, unlike the bandits in "The Creature from the Pit," the Gaztak pirates are engaging and fun. So, even though they could've easily been omitted from the story, they make it a little more fun and interesting.

"Meglos" also benefits from the use of Scene-Sync, which created some nice camera shots that sets the serial apart from others. I know JNT catches a lot of flack for the downfall of Classic *Doctor Who*, but I admire his willingness to try different things, even if not all of them work. With all that said, "Meglos" is a story pregnant with possibilities, and as a result, it is a fun story worthy of being watched several times.

Full Circle (1980)
Writer: Andrew Smith
Script Editor: Christopher H. Bidmead
Director: Peter Grimwade
Producer: John Nathan-Turner

There's part of me that loves "Full Circle" and part of me that is left confused about how it all comes together. Like the previous two serials, there's a good feel to the production, but in the end, it feels incomplete. Whether through poor direction or storytelling, "Full Circle" never comes together as a complete serial. Even Tom and Lalla lack their characteristic spark of excitement and fun. Their performances aren't bad, they just seem uninspired; as if they weren't allowed to act freely. Tom does offer some inspired acting while on the Starliner, but Lalla's possession scenes are stilted and comical. There are also several "death" scenes beyond believability: Decider Nefred supposedly dies from a massive head injury, though there's no sign he was struck in the head. Without devolving into mere complaining, there's a lot to be enjoyed about "Full Circle," but with the advantage of retrospect, there's a lot amiss with *Doctor Who*, and "Full Circle" is one of its symptoms. The introduction of Adric, however, is not one of them. Adric will be inconsistently written during his time on the show, but overall, he's a nice addition to this and other serials.

State of Decay (1980)
Writer: Terrance Dicks
Script Editor: Christopher H. Bidmead
Director: Peter Moffatt
Producer: John Nathan-Turner

Feels like a Classic *Doctor Who* story from the beginning, which of course makes sense, since Terrance Dicks authored the script. What viewers get is the story of the last "real" Vampire, who disappeared into E-Space at the end of the Vampire war against the Time Lords. (Always felt the Vampire vs. Time Lords storyline was underplayed. If you agree, you should probably read the Eighth Doctor novel *Vampire Science*.) The direction feels gothic, and overall, it's a well-done story. Adric's interaction with K-9 is great. In fact, "State of Decay" provides Adric the opportunity to be a shifty con artist, which is the way he was originally conceived. He'll be written inconsistently over his tenure on the show, but Dicks does a nice job of incorporating him into the story.

There are some problematic aspects of the story. Besides Aukon, who reminds me of Gene Simmons, the Vampires are poorly acted. They are stiff and bland. I'm sure they were directed to play their roles as they do, but instead of being creepy, it creates one dimensional characters that are uninteresting. The serial would've been better-off with only Aukon. There's also a scene where Romana needs the Doctor to define a word, which is uncharacteristic of the super intelligent Romana. Even with these hiccups, "State of Decay" is a good story with a fun ending: spaceship blasts off and stabs the creature through the heart—a story that would make even Robin Bland happy.

Warriors' Gate (1981)
Writer: Steve Gallagher
Script Editor: Christopher H. Bidmead
Director: Paul Joyce
Producer: John Nathan-Turner

"Warriors' Gate" has great potential, and what they do with the set is sometimes amazing, but the serial never fully comes together. With the complexity of the story, the serial would've benefited from clearer direction or a simplified script. There are simply too many things happening: there's the main storyline about the Tharils, the end of the E-Space trilogy, and the leaving of Romana and K-9. Somehow they pull it off to varying degrees of success, and as long as you like psychological space dramas, then you should find the serial interesting; but with so much at stake, I expected more. Romana's leaving seems like a tacked-on line at the end, and their return to N-Space is, well, too "normal." The good news is the set and special effects look good throughout the serial, creating a strangeness that makes you feel like you're in E-Space, and at the end you're left with the Doctor and Adric. In fact, Adric's character seems to work best when it's just him and the Fourth Doctor, which won't last for long.

The Keeper of Traken (1981)
Writer: Johnny Byrne
Script Editor: Christopher H. Bidmead
Director: John Black
Producer: John Nathan-Turner

"The Keeper of Traken" is a wonderful story with an intriguing plot that is well-executed. The story introduces several new elements, including a novel approach to re-reintroducing the Master. Johnny Byrne does a superior job crafting mystery with the Keeper and Melkur, John Black creates a real sense of oppression and an Eden-under-attack feel, and the supporting actors rise to the occasion. Tom seems invigorated, and his work with Anthony Ainley's Tremas is delightful, especially if you know Tremas (an anagram) will eventually become the Master. In fact, knowing Tremas will become the Master creates a sense of threat within the story of which the characters are complety unaware. The whole "who will be the Keeper" seems unimportant, in light of what's coming. What is more, viewers are introduced to Nyssa, who is a great companion and would've made a nice long-term companion for the Fourth Doctor. (In addition to her time on the show, she and the Fifth Doctor have some fun adventures on Big Finish.) When all of this is combined, "The Keeper of Traken" remains one of my favorite Tom Baker stories, and I will often suggest it as a good example of Classic *Who.*

Logopolis (1981)
Writer: Christopher H. Bidmead
Script Editor: Christopher H. Bidmead
Director: Peter Grimwade
Producer: John Nathan-Turner

I have mixed feelings about "Logopolis." Part of me really enjoys the serial. We're introduced to Tegan and the Watcher, the Master is back and creating havoc, and the Doctor is out to save the universe. Of course, it all starts with the simple task of repairing the TARDIS's chameleon circuit, but ends with the Master accidently threatening the destruction of the universe. The Doctor and Master agree to work together to fix things, while the Master continues to plot how best to take over Earth and kill the Doctor. In other words, "Logopolis" reckons several classic elements from *Doctor Who*'s past in order to create a fun final romp for Tom.

There's part of me, however, that feels uneasy about the episode. It's hard to really pin down why, but let me offer two possible explanations. Frist, it's Tom's final serial, so simply enjoying the story is difficult. The whole time I'm thinking, "This is Tom's last episode!" As a result, I keep looking towards the future without fully enjoying the present. Second, I feel like they could have come up with a better ending to Tom's tenure. Similar to the First Doctor losing to fatigue, the Fourth Doctor loses to gravity. They could've at least had him sacrifice himself by jumping into the data-stream of the satellite in order to save the universe. Instead, he falls, and so the ending falls flat too.

Even though I don't like how the Fourth Doctor dies, the Doctor's final scene is the most interesting psychological aspect of the show. In one way, the Doctor falling from the satellite dish seems contrived—he's survived much worse. When watching the scene, however, there's a sense that the Doctor could save himself, but chooses instead to fall. What is more, Tom decides to portray the Doctor as tired and exhausted, and shows a sense of relief while he's on the ground dying. To me, Tom's choice to portray the final scene in this way illustrates his behind-the-scenes feelings toward his last season. Sure, he could've fought, stayed on as the Doctor, and probably lasted another ten years, but with all of the changes in cast and production crews, he found himself tired and relieved to go.

Season 18 Summation

Season 18 is difficult to assess. There's just so much going on: Romana and K-9 leave, Tom leaves, there's a new title sequence, and as a result of John Nathan-Turner (JNT) taking over, the show has a new feel. Some of the changes work, and JNT should be lauded for trying to push *Doctor Who* into the future. However, Tom's performances, for whatever the reason, often seem uninspired, and the serials begin to feel incomplete, rushed, or simply confusing. Overall, there are some stellar performances throughout the season, especially from guest stars, and all of the serials contain intriguing concepts and storylines. Nevertheless, all of these features rarely come together at the same time to produce "magical," unforgettable serials. The more I watch the season, the more it becomes apparent that Tom should've left at the end of Season 17, or Williams should've stuck around to end Tom's run on the show. Since I don't have a TARDIS, Season 18 will remain Tom's weakest season as the Doctor.

With that said, there's still plenty of enjoyable *Doctor Who* to be viewed. "The Leisure Hive" ranks number one. It's a great story with lots of twists and turns. "The Keeper of Traken" ranks second. "Traken" gives viewers a great story with fabulous acting, and the full return of the Master. Nyssa serves as a fabulous addition, and the interplay between Tom and Anthony Ainley promises great future fun. Sadly, Ainley (the Master) will only have one episode to battle Tom-as-the-Doctor. Coming in at third is "Logopolis." Tom's last full adventure as the Doctor has its strengths and weaknesses, but overall, it provides a nice farewell to the Fourth Doctor. Sure, there could've been a more meaningful way for the Doctor to die, but the tension of the serial up until the satellite scene, is convincing and strong. I just wish he would've died from something more substantial than a fall from a satellite catwalk.

With its story and great guest appearances, "Meglos" comes in at four. If not for "Logopolis" being the last of Tom's serials, "Meglos" could easily be ranked third, but when all is said and done, it ranks at number four. Terrance Dicks's "State of Decay" ranks fifth. It's a nice story with many classic elements, but it suffers from either stilted acting or uninspired direction. In the end, it creates a new mythos for Doctor Who about the Time Lords' war with Vampires, which is notable in its own right. Thanks, Uncle Terrance. "Full Circle" ranks at six, with "Warriors Gate" ranking at seven.

Season 18 Ranking

1. The Leisure Hive
2. The Keeper of Traken
3. Logopolis
4. Meglos
5. State of Decay
6. Full Circle
7. Warriors' Gate

Recap of Doctor Who Rankings

To make things easier for anyone who wants to see all of the rankings together, and to do your own, here's a recap. The "overall" category is a comparison of each season's winner, not a comparison of all serials. An episode-by-episode comparison is too complicated, and often gives an improper impression that some episodes are worse than they are in reality. Colin Baker made me aware of how this occurs in best-to-worst lists, and I think he's correct. (He's definitely not the worst Doctor, because for me, there is no such thing as a "worst" Doctor. Each Doctor, and each story, is different and loved for different reasons.) Feel free to write your own numbers beside your favorites (unless this is a library book) and tally your own winner.

Season 12

1. Genesis of the Daleks
2. The Ark in Space
3. Revenge of the Cybermen
4. Robot
5. The Sontaran Experiment

Season 13

1. Pyramids of Mars
2. Terror of the Zygons
3. The Brain of Morbius
4. The Android Invasion
5. Planet of Evil
6. The Seeds of Doom

Season 14

1. The Robots of Death
2. The Talons of Weng-Chiang
3. The Deadly Assassin
4. The Hand of Fear
5. The Masque of Mandragora
6. The Face of Evil

Season 15
1. The Sun Makers
2. Image of the Fendahl
3. The Invasion of Time
4. The Invisible Enemy
5. Underworld
6. Horror of Fang Rock

Season 16
1. The Pirate Planet
2. The Stones of Blood
3. The Power of Kroll
4. The Ribos Operation
5. The Armageddon Factor
6. The Androids of Tara

Season 17
1. City of Death
2. Nightmare of Eden
3. Destiny of the Daleks
4. The Creature from the Pit
5. The Horns of Nimon
6. Shada

Season 18
1. The Leisure Hive
2. The Keeper of Traken
3. Logopolis
4. Full Circle
5. Meglos
6. Warriors' Gate
7. State of Decay

Overall Winner from Each Season: The Fourth Doctor's Top 7

1. City of Death
2. Pyramids of Mars
3. Genesis of the Daleks
4. The Robots of Death
5. The Pirate Planet
6. The Sun Makers
7. The Leisure Hive

REVIEW OF SELECTED WORKS

***Nicholas and Alexandra* (1971)**

Besides the Doctor, Grigori Rasputin might be Tom's greatest role. Tom's portrayal is subtle, reserved, and has an ever-present power. Maybe it's his intimate knowledge of sin, faith, and theology, or his bohemian life as a performer, but his portrayal of the *strannik* (wandering monk) Rasputin is gorgeous to watch. Until the advent of the Internet, the only hint of this film was seen in still photos of Tom in make-up. (I remember watching a film about the Romanovs in the mid-80s, but I have no way of knowing if it was this film.) All fans of Tom owe it to themselves to see the film at least once. As a bonus, Tom's performance of the inebriated Rasputin in his final days gives the audience a glimpse into the character who will become the Doctor. Spend some time, learn some history, and be amazed.

***The Canterbury Tales* (1972)**

Not essential watching, even for the most diehard Tom Baker fan. For those who must see it all, Tom is only featured for a few minutes, but during that time, there's full frontal nudity, sexual favors, death, and a little nose-biting.

***The Golden Voyage of Sinbad* (1973)**

Like *Jason and the Argonauts*, *The Golden Voyage of Sinbad* was a marvel for a six-year-old. Excitement, danger, dark arts, and Claymation—what's not to like? I had no idea Tom Baker was the antagonist Prince Koura when I was young, but upon re-watching, he does a great job. Tom exudes a sense of possession and black magic that makes his character believable, especially as he slowly ages. (A precursor of "The Leisure Hive"?) It's no surprise that his performance inspired an invitation to be the Fourth Doctor. The performances of Prince Koura, Grigori Rasputin, and the Doctor illustrate nicely Tom's range as an actor.

***Never Wear Your Wellies in the House and Other Poems to Make You Laugh* (1981)**

Nice to see Tom giving back and helping children in need. *Never Wear Your Wellies…* collects poems from various writers, coupled with drawings from special-needs children. Together they make a delightful book that entertains and delights. You also get a nice short poem from Tom of why you should never wear your wellies in the house.

The Hound of the Baskervilles (1982)

Maybe I was overly optimistic for this production, since the Doctor is sort of an intergalactic Sherlock Holmes, but the serial is uninspired and falls flat. The cinematography is nice, and it makes me want to visit Scotland, but the mystery doesn't feel urgent, and Tom's performance is stilted. He delivers his lines too quickly, without any sort of emotional grounding. Maybe he was trying a different character approach and wanted to avoid the easy trap of playing the Doctor, but it results in a Sherlock with no charm, which provides no reason for viewers to keep watching.

Remington Steele, "Hounded Steele" (1984)

Remington Steele was a favorite at our house when I was a kid. It was always fun to watch, but I was blown away the night I saw Tom Baker appear in an episode. There's nothing especially deep or provocative in the episode, but it's the fun romp you expect from *Remington Steele*. Tom plays an Interpol agent determined to get revenge against a thief who caused him humiliation. Of course, his plan backfires, and he winds up tackled by a dog and arrested. Good times for all!

Doctor Who: The Tom Baker Years (1992)

What a great idea. Let's have Tom watch clips from his old episodes and talk about the people and experiences. What could go wrong? Well, if you know Tom, he has a way of taking you on journey, no matter how mundane the subject matter. Tom's opening explanation is fun, and feels like he has stepped right back into the role of the Doctor. Some of Tom's stories are quite informative, while others offer some naughty insights into the behind-the-scenes exploits of the cast. However, there are times during the special when Tom takes viewers on a mournful journey into life and disappointment (e.g., I can't make friends, I was forgotten, etc.). In the end, Tom's brutal honesty is refreshing and inspiring, and that's one reason I love Tom. He's like jazz. You get lulled into a nice melody, then the tempo and time signature change, then you're struggling to keep and catch up; and by the time you do, he takes you in a different direction. His genuine enthusiasm and candor about the challenges of existence make *The Tom Baker Years* a meaningful viewing experience.

The BBC filmed the special live, so Tom's reactions are sometimes incorrect (the correct information appears at the bottom of the screen), and other times he has no recollection of the episode or what's occurring. For those who have never attended a *Doctor Who* convention, like Gallifrey One, WHOlanta, or Chicago TARDIS, Tom's interactions on film (e.g., "I'm sorry I can't remember or tell you any more") remind me of the type of real life interactions with *Doctor Who* guests and stars. For them, like all of us when we get older, the details of life get fuzzy, and you can either lie and invent "truth," or you can be honest like Tom. As I've tried to show throughout this book, I love Tom's honesty, no matter how aloof some people interpret it to be. Tom talking live reminds me of my own mental engagement with the world, where I'm often lost somewhere between my imagination and the world in which others exist. (And by the way, the new Blu Ray collection featuring the special contains the 90's BBC jingle for VHS releases—dun dun dun, dun dun dun, dun dun dun…)

***Who on Earth is Tom Baker* (1997)**

Love this book. When it was released, I wasn't much of a reader, but for Tom, I sat down and made time to read. I found myself laughing aloud on every page. Full of quirky, strange, and touching stories, Tom takes readers on a journey through his life, which at times seems as fanciful as an episode of *Doctor Who*. If you read the other chapters in this book, you know Tom's autobiography served as the framework for how this book is organized. *Who on Earth is Tom Baker* is one of the few books I have reread several times, and I can't imagine any fan being disappointed. Disgusted, and maybe disturbed, at some stories; but disappointed…never!

***The Boy Who Kicked Pigs* (1999)**

Tom Baker's foray into children's literature would make Neil Gaiman proud. With delightful illustrations by David Roberts, Tom tells the story of a nasty little bugger named Robert Caligari. He kicks pigs! He also does some other pretty vile stuff, but in the end, he is trapped, has his eyes eaten, and dies. In a beautiful display of irreverence, Tom shows off his abilities as a master storyteller. Always fun to curl up with a copy of this when it's dark and scary outside. Shivers, indeed!

***Little Britain* (2003-2007)**

Tom narrates a fake reality show set as a tour guide's perspective of some of the lesser-known aspects of Britain, featuring David Walliams and Matt Lucas. With Matt Lucas in blackface, and several other provocative characters, *Little Britain* is not for everyone. I'll let readers determine the merits of the series, but it is telling that Matt Lucas said he wouldn't make the show knowing what he knows now about humor and the portrayal of others. Regardless, Tom's contribution adds a little charm to this uniquely fun British show, setting the tone for something expectantly irreverent.

Tom Baker Reads *A Christmas Carol* (2012)

If you've never read Charles Dickens's classic *A Christmas Carol*, you really should. Yes, the style takes some getting used to, but Dickens is an excellent writer and it's a great story. Of course, if you're thinking to yourself, "I'm never gonna read it," then you're in luck—you can listen to Tom Baker read it to you. Listening to Tom's version is slowly becoming my own Christmas tradition. Tom delivers a strong performance that makes Dickens's novel come to life, as if he were one of the ghosts of Christmas. As a bonus, the cover is a painting of Tom as Ebenezer Scrooge. Definitely worth the time and money. Wish Tom would read more audio books.

Tom Baker at 80 (2014)

Tom and Nicholas Briggs provide a delightful conversation in "Tom Baker at 80." From the opening seconds, when they discuss Tom's blank notepad, to the closing discussion of how he's "learned nothing" in his 80 years, Tom engages and inspires listeners, while also causing continual laughter. Tom shares insights into getting old, being tolerant and happy, religion, relationships and everything in between. "Tom Baker at 80" gives fans a continuing glimpse into the zaniness that is Tom Baker, which for me, never gets old. I often listen to this interview on days when I'm not feeling so great, and it always lifts me up. Thanks Tom and Nick!

The Fourth Doctor Adventures: Tom Baker's Audio Books

With several audio adventures available, it's hard to cover them all. Instead, I'll speak of them in broad terms. For the most part, if you're a fan of Tom's portrayal of the Fourth Doctor, then you won't be disappointed. There are some caveats. Tom's first series of audios, collected in *Doctor Who: The Nest Cottage Chronicles* ("Hornets' Nest," "Demon Quest," and "Serpent Crest"), don't quite capture the hearts of *Doctor Who*. I often found myself bored and sometimes annoyed by the story and some of the acting (and, of course, the freaking bees). Don't get me wrong, Serpent Crest was clever, especially in light of Tom's previous work as Rasputin, but there are better recordings in which to start one's listening journey.

Fast forward a few years to when Big Finish takes over the audio production of Fourth Doctor stories, and the magic has returned. There are currently ten seasons, several episodes of "Philip Hinchcliffe Presents," and many more one-off stories. Big Finish provides fans with a whole new universe of *Doctor Who*, and it's hard not to purchase them instead of paying my mortgage, but the thrill of hearing Tom be the Doctor again is worth several of my (and your) hard earned dollars.

"The Day of the Doctor" (2013)

I successfully avoided all spoilers leading up to "The Day of the Doctor," and as a result, I was flabbergasted by Tom's appearance. In terms of the story, it seemed like another unnecessary Moffatt-era flourishing to boost the excitement factor (e.g. Clara riding her motorcycle into the TARDIS, Matt

Smith hanging from the TARDIS, etc.), but in this case I didn't mind one bit. I gushed with tears of excitement. Though older, Tom didn't miss a beat. Though "The Five(ish) Doctors Reboot" was probably the best 50th Anniversary tribute, Tom's appearance was the icing on the cake. Maybe it's the Classic Whovian in my soul speaking, but apart from David Tennant's reappearance, when I think 50th Anniversary, I think of "The Five(ish) Doctors Reboot" and the last few minutes of "The Day of the Doctor" when Tom is on screen. Those two things have the most meaning for me, and if Tom hasn't taught me anything else, it is that we should embrace and delight in what we find meaningful. That's a good lesson for anyone and everyone!

THE END

(Until Time and Space Creates a New Beginning)

ABOUT THE AUTHOR

Courtland Lewis is author of *The Real Meaning of Doctor Who*, *Repentance and the Right to Forgiveness*, and co-editor (with Paula Smithka) of *Doctor Who and Philosophy: Bigger on the Inside* and *More Doctor Who and Philosophy: Regeneration Time*. He received his PhD from the University of Tennessee and is Associate Professor of Philosophy at Pellissippi State Community College.

Also Available From

kOZMIC CLASSICS

THE TIME MACHINE

125th Anniversary Edition

A gentleman inventor makes the wild claim to a collection of friends that he has created a machine that gives him the ability to travel through time. He recounts a tale of his visit to in Earth's extreme future, in which humanity has evolved into two extreme and distinct races—the angelic, Eloi, and the monstrous, subterranean Morlocks—who represent the extremes of the duality of human nature. First published in 1895, The Time Machine is a foundational classic in the realm of science fiction that extrapolates on the unevenness of the Victorian class system. This 125th Anniversary Edition includes: * The original short story, "The Chronic Argonauts," which Wells later expanded into the novel* The complete The Time Machine novel by H. G. Wells, including a section of text that was not included in either the original British or American publications* A newly-written essay by Dr. Lisa Yaszek, Professor of Science Fiction Studies at Georgia Tech, tracing the development between the two works.

978-17340840-3-0 $8.00 www.kozmicpress.com

Printed in Great Britain
by Amazon

23569835R00066